5: DESERTED VILLAGES IN NORFOLK

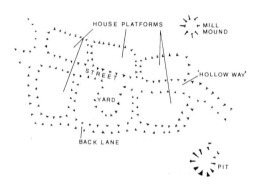

Alan Davison
in collaboration with the Norfolk Museums Service

Maps: Alan Davison, Poppyland Publishing

Photographs:
Norfolk Air Photographs Library - Derek A. Edwards
University of Cambridge Committee for Aerial Photography
Poppyland Photos

Cover photo: Holkham Hall, standing where a village once stood.
(Norfolk Air Photographs Library - Derek A. Edwards)

Contents

Other titles in the Norfolk Origins series:
1: Hunters to First Farmers (Published 1981)
2: Roads and Tracks (Published 1983)
3: Celtic Fire and Roman Rule (Published 1987)
4: The North Folk: Angles, Saxons and Danes (Published 1990)

Text © 1996 Alan Davison
Maps and Drawings © 1996 Alan Davison
ISBN: 0 946148 51 1
Published by Poppyland Publishing, North Walsham, Norfolk 1996
Cover design by Printing Services (Norwich) Ltd.
Printed by Printing Services (Norwich) Ltd.

Warning
Reference to or representation of a site, track, road should not be taken that such a site, track or road can be seen or may be visited. In many cases sites are on private land.

Introduction

Norfolk is a county of villages, villages which are usually small and of many shapes and forms. Some of their features have long been noticed: isolated churches, villages with more than one church, and the occasional ruined church. Once there were more villages; just how many is difficult to say as research reveals more and more. An increasingly complicated picture of rural settlement is emerging as investigation continues, and the complications are multiplied by regional differences. Norfolk, though flat, has a variety of landscapes. They include the wetlands of Fenland, Broadland and the river valleys, the dry sandy Breckland, areas of heavy chalky boulder clay in central and south Norfolk, the Goodsand of the north-west and the loamy soils of the north-east. In each we may expect to find something different.

What is a Deserted Village?

For thousands of years Norfolk has been settled and people have left traces of their dwellings. The Roman occupation alone lasted almost 400 years and in that time many rural settlements existed. Their abandoned sites are often to be found in our fields and, with Iron Age and even earlier sites, could be seen as 'deserted villages'. While accepting this, we will take the beginnings of English settlement (about AD450) as the starting point of our story.

Among our existing villages are some showing clear signs of having once been much larger. These are called 'shrunken' rather than 'deserted' villages, but their vanished streets or lost hamlets have certainly been deserted. Others have been shifted or have drifted from their original positions; occasionally a parish may contain more than one earlier site of a still-existing village. The abandoned sites are obviously 'deserted'. Some villages are completely deserted apart from a church, often ruined, and a farm or solitary house still bearing the old name. For some this is the only true desertion and it would be difficult to quarrel with this if all our villages had been of simple compact (nucleated) shape. In Norfolk the pattern of rural settlement is so diverse that hard and fast distinctions are difficult to make. There will be no attempt to do this in the following pages.

INTRODUCTION
Past Knowledge

The destruction of villages did not go unnoticed at the time. The spate of desertions which took place at the end of the Middle Ages and in the sixteenth century caused such disquiet that the government tried to take action to stem it. 'An acte agaynst pullyng doun of Tounes' in 1489 was followed by further acts and a Commission of Inquiry in 1517, all designed to stop the destruction. They met with only partial success. The Commission was not given power to enquire into acts committed before Michaelmas 1488, and powerful land-owning interests were able to put a brake on any reform. Kett's rebellion of 1549 was a local expression of hostility to the actions of landlords. Villagers who lost their livelihoods were in danger of becoming 'loose and wandering people'. One Tudor historian compiled a list of deserted villages and other writers passed comments in their works. One of Shakespeare's characters, a fisherman, described the 'land whales' who swallowed whole parishes with the churches, steeples and bells.

After this, desertions were less frequent and attracted less notice among the great and the learned. An exception is Goldsmith's poem 'The Deserted Village', first printed in 1770, which described another kind of desertion - clearance to make a park. He called his village 'Sweet Auburn' but it is known to have been Nuneham Courtney in Oxfordshire. Of the subject of the poem he said that he had taken the greatest care in four or five years' journeying about the countryside to be sure of his facts. Otherwise, memories of desertion persisted in popular legends, usually inaccurate.

Modern Studies

Until the 1940s many historians maintained that deserted villages were few. However, work by W G Hoskins and M W Beresford in Leicestershire, Warwickshire and Yorkshire was to show that they were many. Beresford and John Hurst began excavating at Wharram Percy in Yorkshire, work that went on for 40 years, while Hurst launched the Deserted Medieval Village Research Group. The first work in Norfolk was done by Keith Allison whose study of the subject was published in 1955; it included a list of deserted places. Peter Wade-Martins followed with surveys of villages in the

Launditch Hundred (1967-70), and excavations at Thuxton (1963-4), with Lawrence Butler, at Grenstein (1965-6) and North Elmham (1967-72). The Norfolk Archaeological Rescue Group completed and published descriptions of 14 deserted sites (1982, 1988) and work by groups and individuals has continued. Enough has been learned to show that, in Norfolk, desertion is very complicated and much remains to be done, both in the field and among documents.

THE EARLIEST VILLAGES

Early ('Pagan') Saxon Norfolk

The idea was long current that the Angles who settled in the eastern counties were responsible for founding the villages of today. Students of place names produced lists of 'early' and 'later' names which were said to mark the progress of settlement. 'Early' certain names may be, but they probably do not date back to the time of the first settlers. Others may have come into use at a late date, replacing ones now unknown. Research has shown that it is unsafe to think that all present villages are in sites chosen by the earlier waves of settlers. Unfortunately, they left comparatively few signs of their habitations; we know more about their cemeteries. Where settlements have been found they seem to have been in small clusters scattered around within the bounds of present parishes. They had no plan or street system but were merely vague groups of huts. West Stow in Suffolk has an example. It was abandoned in the mid-seventh century. The only certain 'Pagan' site in Heckingham, near Loddon, is on a sandy knoll overlooking a stream, close to a very small Romano-British settlement and quite far from the later village. Two sites of the period in Loddon are similarly positioned. Two of the three have never been settled since.

Middle Saxon Norfolk (cAD650 to cAD850)

Sites of this period are identified by the presence of Ipswich-type Ware, a kind of pottery named after the place where it is known to have been mass-produced in this period. Finds made are, in many cases, from entirely new sites such as Hay Green in Terrington St Clement. In the Launditch hundred settlements of this period occur close to churches. In Heckingham, concentrations of Ipswich-type Ware are found near the church, well away from the earlier site. There seems to have been a general shifting of settlement.

Late Saxon and Early Medieval Villages (cAD850 to AD1150)

Finds made by field walkers have shown that some villages of this period were simply enlargements from a Middle Saxon core. In others some shifting from earlier sites had occurred. In Heckingham centres of activity had begun to move short distances in various directions. In neighbouring Hales, despite careful searching, no sign

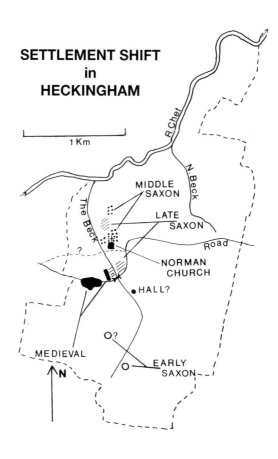

SETTLEMENT SHIFT in HECKINGHAM

1 Km

R.Chet

N.Beck

The Beck

MIDDLE SAXON

LATE SAXON

?

Road

NORMAN CHURCH

HALL?

O?

O

MEDIEVAL

N

EARLY SAXON

of Middle Saxon occupation has been found and there are only small scattered clusters of Late Saxon or Early Medieval settlement, most of them distant from the church. However, in 1086 the Domesday survey recorded a substantial number of people for Hales and there is no simple explanation for the discrepancy. Excavations of some deserted medieval villages outside Norfolk gave no sign of Late Saxon occupation. The people said to be living there by Domesday Book must have dwelt somewhere nearby. We must be prepared for the same to be true of some Norfolk villages.

The Lost Domesday 'Vills'

Some 'vills' which were named in the Domesday Book subsequently disappeared from the records. Some may have been absorbed by more successful neighbours and so may still exist as nameless parts

THE PROBABLE SITE OF TOIMERE

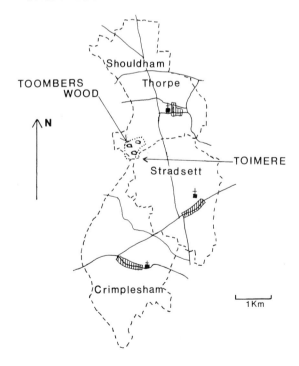

of an existing village. Wica in Guiltcross hundred is a good example of this, it became a manor within Garboldisham. Perhaps some vanished places had been newly-founded settlements which soon failed. Others may have been flourishing in earlier times and, after a period of decline, were about to die. There are places which appear to be lost beyond hope of discovery though some clue may exist in some medieval document that awaits the searcher. 'Risinga' in Grimshoe hundred is one of these; it seems to have been not far from surviving villages near the edge of the Fens. Sites of others are known within a little. Toimere (Toombers) was a tiny place in 1086 and was not mentioned again in any national record. Minor place names in fourteenth century charters and a rental of the manor of Garboisthorpe in Shouldham Thorpe make it plain that Toimere must have been somewhere in the north-west corner of Stradsett parish.

THE MEDIEVAL VILLAGES

Domesday Book was the first written account of English settlements. Recent investigations have shown that, before 1086, the pattern of settlement in Norfolk, as in many other places, had already undergone changes. More were to come. From the centuries after Domesday, more and more documents survive to support the work of the archaeologist. Before we follow the story further it is necessary to describe the composition and workings of a medieval village, remembering always that such places in Norfolk were very variable in form.

The Houses
Each house with its surroundings was called a toft; other names which appear in documents are messuage and curtilage for the house and its immediate land. Attached to a toft would have been a piece of enclosed land, small enough to be cultivated by hand and known as a croft. The two pieces together made a rough rectangle which was bounded by banks and ditches with hedges on the banks to keep out wandering animals. Usually there would be a division between toft and croft. On aerial photographs of earthworks they often show up quite clearly. Some may be irregular in shape and size, suggesting haphazard growth. Other groups of a regular form hint at some stage of organised planning in the village's history.

Even at ground level these old property boundaries may survive visibly in undisturbed grassland; distinct ridges of this kind can still be seen at Waterden and at Rougham.

Building stones other than flints and other field stones are scarce, particularly in eastern Norfolk, so that most homes were made of materials which have not survived. Excavations at Thuxton and Grenstein have given some information about the nature of medieval peasant houses in Norfolk but firmer knowledge can only come from further excavations. At Thuxton some of the walls of houses had foundations of flints and erratics (stones brought by Ice Age glaciers). The walls were made of mud or clay strengthened by posts; in some houses walls had been laid directly on the ground surface. Timber for building was no longer plentiful by the thirteenth century but wattle frameworks could be used in walling. Fire-hardened daub with marks of wattle still plain to see has been found by field walkers at the deserted village site of Bodney.

The roofs were supported by posts. Placing these upright in post-holes would have meant regular replacement as they rotted in the ground. To prevent this, posts were placed on pads of clay or flints on the surface of the ground. Roofs were thatched with straw. Floors were of beaten chalky clay; often clay floors are all that survives to show where houses once stood. Fire-cracked flints spread on such floors mark the positions of hearths. Smoke from the fires escaped through smokeholes in the roofs. Inside, the houses were simply partitioned. Outside yards were often cobbled with flints to withstand the trampling of animals and the passage of carts. Smaller buildings constructed in similar fashion, often with hipped roofs rather than gables, were for storage or for animals. No evidence has been found to say that animals and humans lived under the same roof in East Anglia. One building in Thuxton had horses' heads buried under the threshold; perhaps they were protective magic for horses stabled there. Within the toft there would have been pits dug and filled in from time to time - cesspits, rubbish pits and pits for holding water. Drinking water may have come from the village well, as at Rougham, where the common well was in the main street not far from the surviving pump.

The earliest surviving maps do show houses which can be seen as later versions of medieval ones; very few are shown as half-timbered. Most were single-storeyed, one- or two- roomed buildings and hardly any had chimney stacks. Apart from changes in style, which might be expected over centuries, the perishable materials of which houses were made meant much repairing and rebuilding. Bricks began to appear in the thirteenth and fourteenth centuries at Thuxton, but here and at Grenstein they were not used in quantity. Roofing tiles also replaced thatch to some extent.

The Contents of Houses

Finds from excavations and from the surface give only a limited picture of a medieval household. Iron objects found include things used in building, such as nails, staples and angle-irons, tools such as knives, sickles, gouges and spoon-bits, and items from furnishings and fittings, such as keys, padlocks, hinges and hinge-pivots. Copper alloy pieces include buckles, strap ends, animal bells and bits of cauldron. The commonest stone objects found are fragments of lava querns imported from the Rhineland, of mortars, and of whetstones, many of which appear to have come from Norway.

Pottery finds are more numerous. Fragments of cooking pots and bowls are frequent surface finds on village sites. Those of Late Saxon or Early Medieval date such as Thetford-type Ware or St Neots-type Ware may be present but are usually scarce by comparison with later types. Much medieval pottery is coarse unglazed ware, but glazed forms are quite numerous, many of them being made at Grimston near King's Lynn. Imported pottery from the continent or from other parts of England can also be found in small quantities. They include stonewares from the Rhineland, but most of these are from later centuries.

Inventories made when persons died survive but they date from the period after the Middle Ages and give, perhaps, a picture of wealthier, more elaborately equipped households than those of medieval peasants. An inventory of the household goods of a man who died at Beachamwell in 1592 and who was a yeoman (roughly equivalent to the earlier freeman) mentions little in the way of furniture: one chair, one table, two forms and some stools, as well as a cupboard and two coffers. Utensils included two brass pots, a skillet, a candlestick, a chafing-dish, six pewter dishes and a salt, tongs, bellows, two pairs of pot-hooks and a lantern, a spit and two 'cobirons', two kettles, a pan, four bottles and six 'treen' (wooden) dishes. This does not give details of rooms in the house or outhouses. A comparable but later inventory from Kilverstone lists rooms as a hall, a chamber, a kitchen and an upper chamber. Wills of the sixteenth century sometimes make provision for dependants to stay on in 'the backhouse'. The backhouse may have been a lean-to built on to the main house or an outhouse; the arrangement seems rather like the modern 'granny flat'. Some messuages were subdivided. In Kilverstone in 1471 a man had a room in the eastern end of a messuage with right of separate access for life.

The Street

The village street was a track, probably rather irregular, worn deep by men, animals and cart wheels. On clay soils, deep ruts were worn in wet weather. Some were uncovered by excavations at Thuxton and Grenstein. At Grenstein the street was surfaced with well-worn flints and bordered by drainage ditches. There had been attempts to repair the surface which was about six metres in width. At Thuxton there was also flint metalling and successive layers of surface. Even on sandy sites, like Caldecote, ditches flanked the street. Sometimes a street would open out into a narrow green bounded by ditches and banks; this would serve as common grazing. With rows of tofts and crofts facing the street it became necessary to reach the backs of crofts. Back lanes parallel to the street were made and, if the village grew, turned into true streets. Some small enclosures by the street had no houses. These, pasture or cultivated ground, were called pightles. From the street a network of tracks and paths led away to the fields and to other villages.

The Church

Once the site for a church was chosen it is almost certain that, despite many changes, it would remain in that place; exceptions did occur but they were few. What is less certain is the date of the earliest building. We have already seen that in some villages a Middle Saxon occupation site was close to the church. The village then may not have had a church. If it did it was probably made of wood. Some Saxon churches, known as minsters, were centres from which priests served a district. A church of Middle Saxon time found at Brandon in Suffolk was wooden, and some of the churches listed in Domesday were probably made of wood also. All Saints' church, Barton Bendish, demolished in the eighteenth century, was one of two recorded in 1086. Excavation showed that the first traceable church was built on an existing graveyard of the eleventh century, probably after the Conquest. It seems likely that the graveyard belonged to a lost wooden church, quite possibly the one mentioned in 1086.

Domesday Book records churches in 217 villages, but other evidence brings the total closer to 300 at least; there were certainly more. Many were founded, endowed and owned by the lords of the villages, hence their listing in Domesday among their holdings. Villages with more than one lord could have more than one church.

Many 'Saxon' churches are better described as 'Saxo-Norman' because native workmen still used old styles when building for new lords. Most were simple buildings but in later years churches were enlarged and new styles concealed or replaced the original form. Often aisles were added. These may have been for a growing village but it is just as likely that they were meant to show wealth, to allow for processions and additional altars, or to hold family tombs.

Manors

Many Norfolk villages, in 1086, were already divided among two or more lords. Even if there had been just one lord, later divisions of land altered this. Sub-division became so frequent that, in 1290, it was forbidden because of the problems it caused to the feudal organisation of the country. Illington, one manor in 1086, had been divided by 1302 among a dozen lords, most of them minor; a few years later there were just two manors, marked until recently by the remains of two moats. The lands belonging to a manor were not confined to the parish but could extend into neighbouring parishes. Each manorial lord could hold his own courts of law.

The earliest manor house was probably near the church and of wooden construction. More substantial materials such as flint or, later, bricks and tiles were used in replacement. Brick walling and floor tiles were found at an excavated manor house at Hempstead; the tiles could be dated 1300-1350.

Moats began to appear after about 1150. Not all manor houses were moated and not all moats surrounded manor houses. Moats were usually rectangular and contained water, though some were dry. There are many on the wetter clay lands of central and south Norfolk. Some were fed by streams, others relied on ground water. Their purpose is not clear. They would have served as protection from small bands of robbers but not from a serious force; they could, on clay soils, have provided drainage for the house platform inside; they could have served as sources of fresh fish. It is quite likely that they were built to impress - a symbol of status. By about 1350 they were passing from fashion although some continued to be made.

Fish ponds were sometimes near manor houses. Some, like three at Bodney, were rectangular hollows. Others were linked together in more complicated groups.

Mills

Over 300 Norfolk vills had mills in 1086. Many had more than one. The Barshams had at least nine among them. Domesday mills were water-powered, so their construction must have meant the building of dams and channels. They were a source of profit to lords whose tenants had to pay in kind for the grinding of grain.

Windmills appeared in the later twelfth century. They were post mills of simple form. Their advantage was that they could be built at any place open to the winds. The post was fixed and braced upright in a mound. In 1478 two oak trees were needed for the repair of a post mill in the now deserted village of Hargham, one for the post, the other for the axle-tree.

Fields, Commons and Woods

It is not known how the fields were worked in earlier centuries, but by the medieval period a system of open-field farming existed. It was not a static system but was slowly changing and evolving. The arable was in a number of large fields (the number varied from place to place) and sub-divided into areas of differing sizes called, misleadingly, furlongs. Each furlong was divided into strips, some manorial (demesne), some worked by the peasants. Various forms of rotation involving fallow were in use. Some fields were known as 'Infield' and were more intensively used. The rest were 'Outfield'. In order to operate a rotation a system of shifts was used. A shift was an area devoted to one crop or to fallow, regardless of the boundaries of strips, furlongs or fields. Another feature was the fold course, the right to graze animals over stubbles, fallow and heaths, held by lords and some peasants. By the end of the Middle Ages lords had begun to monopolise this right. Enclosure of parts of the fields gathered pace towards the end of the period. Meadows lay in damper, low-lying ground and were also doled out in strips. It must be noted that the situation and practice varied from one part of Norfolk to another.

Commons became increasingly important as more land was ploughed for food. Though they belonged to the manor, tenants had rights, particularly of grazing. Each tenanted holding had a stint or fixed number of animals which could be put on the common. This was vital in summer when fallows gave the only other grazing. In autumn the position was eased for stubble could be grazed in shack-time. Some commons lay on higher ground, such as heaths or clay lands. Low commons lay in wetter situations. Some, inter-commons, were shared between parishes.

The limited Domesday woodlands were mainly on the clay lands of central Norfolk. Medieval woods were bounded by banks and ditches and were exploited regularly. They were of mixed species and consisted of coppice and larger trees. They were usually located in a distant part of a parish, though many parishes had little or no woodland. Alder carr in wet valleys was also valued for coppicing.

The People

The Norfolk people recorded in Domesday were classed as sokemen, freemen, villeins, bordars and serfs. The distinction between sokemen and freemen must often have been small. Both were free and were numerous in Norfolk. However, Tom Williamson has pointed to a difference between them. Sokemen were associated with parts of ancient estates and were taxed through them, while

Freemen paid their own taxes and were more directly linked to higher authority. The meaning of 'bordar' is not clear and serfs were a dwindling group. In medieval times village population, apart from the manorial household and clergy, fell into two groups - freemen and villeins. A freeman was often as poor as a villein but had the right to appeal to royal courts for justice against his lord. He put himself under the protection of the lord in return for certain services, and so long as they were performed could not be evicted. A freeman could leave his holding. A villein held his land by labour services on the lord's land. The lord owned the villein, his land and his possessions, and land could be sold or granted to another lord with the villein and his family. He was not free to leave the manor unless he paid a fine.

As time passed the freeman, or franklin, became the yeoman of the sixteenth century. The villein or bondman later paid rent instead of services and evolved into the copyhold tenant - one who held his land from the lord by copy of the court roll entry recording his admission to the holding. Often a lord would live elsewhere and his bailiff would look after the manor. Towards the end of the period a manor might be at farm (rented or leased) to a tenant.

THE MEDIEVAL POPULATION

Domesday Book tells much about population, but not enough. The people numbered were heads of household; we have to guess how many there were in an 'average' household. There are signs that many were not counted and that, in the course of adapting the returns used to compile Domesday, errors crept in. Various estimates suggest that the population of England was at least one million, that 1.5 million would be a reasonable total and that it might have been two millions. Norfolk seems to have been a densely populated county with over 20 people recorded per square mile in parts of the south-east and east. Judging by the number of plough-teams of oxen per square mile, the eastern half of Norfolk was more intensively cultivated and that parts of the south-east and of Flegg were especially so. Only in Breckland and Fenland were there less than ten people recorded per square mile.

After 1086 the English population grew rapidly. It is not possible to decide on an exact figure. Some say it had risen by about 300 per cent, others suggest seven millions by 1300 when growth ceased, others estimate 3.5 millions. Tax lists do not give all households as those not liable were omitted, and there were evasions. Poll Tax lists do not always tally with information from other documents. Those of 1377 show that Norfolk had a rural population of at least forty people over 14 years of age to the square mile. Field evidence for this in Norfolk can be seen in the expansion of existing villages from Late Saxon cores, as at Grenstein, the creation of new hamlets and of isolated farmsteads.

More mouths meant more pressure on land. More land went under the plough; inroads were made into surviving woodland and commons and 'wastes'. Such intakes were called 'assarts' from a Medieval Latin word meaning 'to pull up'. The curving or lobed boundaries of late-surviving woods and commons show where 'bites' of cultivated land had been taken from them. 'Breche', which is quite frequent among medieval field names, means 'newly broken-in land'. As eastern Norfolk was already densely-populated in 1086 opportunities there for assarting had come to an end by the late twelfth century so that further expansion had to be by more intensive use of cultivated land. In the Norfolk Fenland, in contrast, new lands were still being reclaimed and settled.

Common Edge Settlements

As the rural population increased, so did pressure on land and food supplies. The peasants had to rely more heavily on animal products and so the commons became vital for grazing. Quite large areas of common land still existed as late as 1797 when they were shown on Faden's map of Norfolk. It seems that Norfolk lords had less strict control over their tenants and so it was possible for people, especially free tenants, to settle on the margins of common lands. This sometimes resulted in complete abandonment of the original village site in favour of a new one bordering a common. In other cases, the main village survived but a green-side hamlet developed as well. Over later centuries changes could occur in such a way that the main village gradually vanished leaving the hamlet to bear the village name. In other instances the main villages remained while once-flourishing green-side communities disappeared. Only the pottery scatters left for the field-walker to find betray their former existence.

Longham is an outstanding example of common-edge migration since there was a two-stage movement to its present site. Pottery found near the isolated church shows that a Middle Saxon settlement there had expanded by Late Saxon times. In medieval times there was a shift southwards to the edge of Southhall Green where 16 groups of buildings became established by the thirteenth and fourteenth centuries. Two moated manor houses were built close by. Southhall Green was connected by a narrow passage of common leading north-eastwards to Kirtling Common. In the late fifteenth century movement to Kirtling Common had begun and was well established in the next century. By the nineteenth century the move was complete and Southhall Green had been abandoned.

CHANGING LONGHAM

after P. Wade–Martins

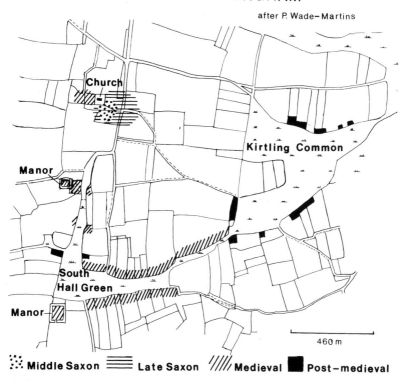

Church

Kirtling Common

Manor

South Hall Green

Manor

460 m

:·: Middle Saxon   ≡≡≡ Late Saxon   ///// Medieval   ■ Post–medieval

At Rougham colonisation of the margins of Bradmere Green to the north-west of the present village began about AD1100. Although nothing exists there now, it seems that settlement was on opposite sides of the green.

At Hales the first signs of activity around Hales Green were on the eastern (Hales) side where small amounts of Thetford-type and early medieval pottery, dateable to the early twelfth century, have been found at several points. By the thirteenth century the eastern side of the green and the western (Loddon) side, where a manorial site was established at Hales Hall, were intensively settled. Today, a few scattered houses and farms, including part of a very late medieval replacement of the medieval Hales Hall, still occupy sites on both sides of the green. The arable land in between them contains bands bordering the green where pottery is plentiful.

The parish of Sporle has a large southern prong which once included Cotes Common, the western end of a large common, shown on Faden's map, extending eastwards through Necton to West Bradenham. Documentary evidence and field-walking finds show that the western and southern edges of the common in Sporle, North Pickenham and part of Holme Hale, were settled at various scattered points during the thirteenth and fourteenth centuries although some twelfth century pottery occurred at one site. Another site named in documents, Petygards, took its name from a family who lived there and was of some consequence; there are remains of a small moat. This common-edge settlement was called Cotes and it lingered on in some form into the sixteenth and early seventeenth centuries. One farmhouse with its buildings remains near the site of Petygards. All else has gone.

In Breckland large areas of heathland occupied the higher lands between the river valleys. Because they were so dry the edges of these heathland grazings were not settled. Better watered pastures along the floors of the valleys offered opportunities for expansion. Illington is a very small parish in eastern Breckland consisting only of an isolated church, a hall, a farm and a few scattered houses. It lies on the southern side of a little valley drained by a small stream flowing eastwards to the Thet. The original village in the eleventh century lay near the church. By the thirteenth century it had moved

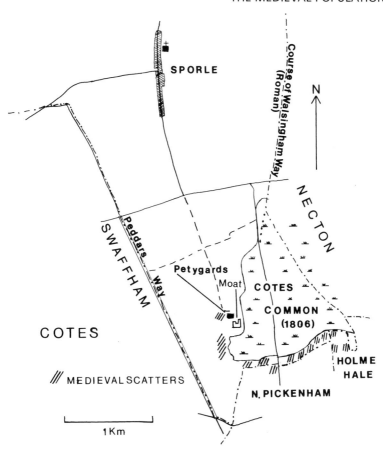

towards the valley floor where there was damp common pasture. A moated manor house was built there. A separate line of dwellings also grew up at this time further to the east of the church along a track following the edge of the wet pastures. This hamlet was called Methlond and it survived, in part, until the end of the sixteenth century. Much further west, also along the edge of pasture land, another street, probably called West End, grew up in the thirteenth century. A little apart from it was a second moated manor house. Only a farm remains at West End. The Hall and some of the cottages are scattered over the site of the main village and its thirteenth century extension.

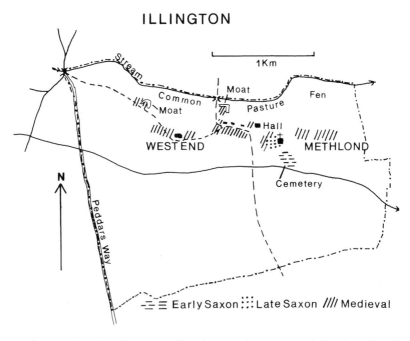

ILLINGTON

Shifts of this kind, especially those which have left the church isolated, have long been a mystery. Those seeking an explanation have turned to the catastrophe which finds a place in folk memory and in history books. It is usually argued that, after the Black Death, the people moved to a fresh site away from the infection of the old one; it is a temptingly easy explanation. However, the Black Death reached Norfolk in 1349 and, as seen by the examples given here, the movements had begun in the twelfth and were at their height in the thirteenth century, long before the coming of the pestilence. Even the second shift at Longham came a very long time after 1349. Clearly the Black Death has to be ruled out as a reason for these movements. It was the pressing need for access to common pasture which seems to have been the cause.

Declining Numbers

After 1300 population declined. The fourteenth century was one of difficulties and downright disaster. It brought an abrupt end to the growth of earlier centuries. The arrival of bubonic plague in England in 1348 and the resulting death roll is a well-known landmark, but there is some evidence that decline had begun much nearer 1300. As there are no figures for the population there will always be argument about the effect that the various incidents and changes had.

As a background to other events climatic changes also had some influence. A long period of warm, dry, stable conditions had ended by 1300, being succeeded by a time of marked variation. Between 1310 and 1350 there were years of extremes. On average it was much colder and there were some years when rain was excessive. It seems likely that Norfolk in some years within this period, had more rain-bearing winds from the North Sea. In England as a whole, abnormal rainfall caused harvests to fail; 1315 and 1316 were bad years when harvests were poor and there is evidence that food was short. Accompanying the poor harvests were outbreaks of sheep murrain. In the years between 1319 and 1321, when some harvests again failed, there were outbreaks of disease among cattle. In any case, it is likely that many cattle had been killed for food when crops failed. Food shortages must have made the spread of epidemics easy among people weakened by poor diet.

Bubonic plague reached Norfolk early in 1349. The death toll was very great but what proportion of the population died is the subject of much argument. The disruption caused by the pestilence often meant that records were not properly kept and so useful information was not passed down. Most authorities settle for a conventional estimate of about one third of whatever the total population was, but some say over one-half while others belittle the effect and suggest one-fifth. Neither of these extremes is likely except in an odd instance. Whatever the true figure was it left a deep impression on people who were quite accustomed to life being brief and harsh. A physician of the time called it 'the grete dethe' because it affected everyone; 'Black Death' was a name given long after for no clear reason. In Norfolk some manorial court records for 1349 survive. Those of Kempstone and Hilborough carry dismal tallies of properties made vacant by death. Mortality among Norfolk parish priests was very great. Bishop Bateman of Norwich founded Trinity Hall, in Cambridge, in order to make good losses among the clergy.

The Black Death has caught popular imagination and drawn attention away from further outbreaks of pestilence, some very serious and less well recorded. These were in 1361-2, 1368-9, 1375-6 and a fifth, almost as great as the first, in 1390-1. Some believe that other diseases may have been responsible in some cases. The outbreaks probably varied in intensity from place to place.

Because of the numerous deaths much land became untenanted and, if no heirs remained alive, was distributed among the living. These might have been surviving inhabitants or people who had grasped the chance to move from a poorer place. Labour was scarce and wages and prices rose. Some lords, desperate for labour, stopped cultivating their demesnes and let them to tenants. Some converted to pastoral farming which needed less labour. Others tried to exact the maximum labour dues from villeins. Lords and well-to-do peasants who required labour wanted to keep down wages, and statutes limiting wages attempted to do this. There was thus growing discord between the various sections of the community. Matters were not helped by more harvest failures and by cattle murrain. It was from this uneasy background, aggravated by the imposition of a series of Poll Taxes, that the Rising of 1381 began.

That most villages must have shrunk is obvious. Untenanted crofts would have been joined to others still occupied and outlying farmsteads may have been abandoned. However, fieldwalkers discovering these ploughed-over sites and finding concentrations of pottery consisting of nothing later than the fourteenth century cannot say for certain that it was plague which brought them to an end.

THE CAUSES OF DESERTION: SOME SUGGESTIONS

Soil Exhaustion and the Retreat from Poorer Soils

The idea that poor soils may have been the reason why some villages were abandoned has been put forward. It is a tempting explanation for early desertions in areas of light soils like Breckland. Some support does come from contemporary comments. In 1394 permission to demolish one of two churches at Blo Norton was sought. The reasons given were pestilences, mortalities, barrenness of lands, ruin of buildings, malice of the times, and, especially, the poverty and fewness of parishioners. The church of St Margaret was duly demolished while St Andrew's remains. Pressure on land resources could lead to soil exhaustion on poorer land but medieval cultivators maintained soil fertility by crop rotations which included legumes such as beans, peas and vetches, as field names show. Manuring by cartage and by the pasturing of flocks over arable land was practised. In Rougham such field names as Marledlond (1292), Marlewong (1328), Manimarlepittes (1297) and Stannardesmarlepit (1275) are good examples, and names referring to loam pits are also quite common. It is difficult to define 'marginal land' as it is possible to adapt farming to suit soils and it is known that thirteenth century Breckland peasants were better off than those on more fertile lands nearby. It is thus unlikely that poor soils alone could bring about desertion. Combined with other factors the quality of soils may well have played a part in desertion, and detailed investigation of the presence or absence of trace elements which may have had a direct bearing on the wellbeing of crops and animals is needed. Also of interest are the reactions of different soils, particularly clays, to variations in climate.

Environmental Changes

Physical

Coastal erosion has removed some villages. Eccles is the best example; the foundations of its church are sometimes laid bare on

The remains of the church at Eccles on the beach at the beginning of the twentieth century. (Poppyland Collection)

23

the shore by the scouring of the sea. Little Waxham is believed to have been lost in the same way, while Shipden, mentioned in Domesday, was probably a forerunner of Cromer. Places lost in this way were destroyed rather than deserted.

Changes of sea level may have affected settlements in low-lying places. Cyclical fluctuations have occurred on top of a general rise in sea level. From a low level at about AD 700 sea level rose to a maximum at about AD 1300 and led to drainage problems in river valleys and to the flooding of Broadland peat-diggings. Some early medieval sites on floors of valleys in Loddon, Sisland and Heckingham were abandoned about this time.

Climatic Changes

The unstable conditions of the fourteenth and early fifteenth centuries brought periods of cooler, wetter weather, separated by more normal years. On hilly ground even a small fall in average temperatures might make crop-growing difficult, and the cultivation of higher land and some settlements in south-eastern Scotland were abandoned. Norfolk is much lower but the increased rainfall and strong northerly winds experienced there in later medieval times, as demonstrated by Professor Lamb, may have made difficulties on clay soils where surface drainage is less good. Manorial court rolls show that at Rougham, Hockham and Kempstone tenants were in trouble for not maintaining ditches in the early fifteenth century. Drainage ditches were dug around houses and the upcast soil helped to raise the house platforms still visible in earthworks. It has been suggested that Grenstein, on an exposed site on heavy boulder clay, is an example of a late colonisation which was deserted in the fifteenth century. The implication that a colder, wetter trend in climate might have brought difficulty to a struggling settlement is clear.

The possibility that wetter conditions experienced in Norfolk in the fourteenth and fifteenth centuries may have had some link with greater interest in sheep rearing in preference to arable farming has also been suggested recently. The actions of landlords who ran large flocks will be discussed later. The part played by climatic change, if any, needs to be studied further.

The storms which occurred in later medieval times exaggerated troubles for certain low-lying settlements. The medieval chronicler John of Oxenede recorded a storm surge in 1287 which covered large areas with sea water. In Hickling Priory the water stood over a foot above the high altar; two courageous canons stayed to lead horses to safety in the dormitory. There are records of flooding in east Norfolk in 1340 and, in 1343, Langley Abbey informed the Pope that income had been reduced by floods. St Benet's Abbey appealed similarly in the following year. From West Norfolk there is other evidence. In about 1271 the church of West Lynn was destroyed by the sea and rebuilt on higher ground. The Benedictine Nunnery at Thetford is said to have been excused tax in the fifteenth century partly because of losses by flooding among its possessions in the Deanery of Cranwich; this included land on the fen edge and the Little Ouse and Wissey valleys.

Apart from coastal destruction and possible limited re-siting on higher ground, it is unlikely that environmental changes were solely responsible for desertions. At most they may have added weight to other factors in some places.

Pestilence

For many the Black Death has been clear favourite as the cause of desertion. Many villages must have suffered grievous losses and experienced decline to some extent. The shapes of Norfolk villages, many of them straggling in the first place, make it much harder to detect its effects. Concentrations of medieval pottery found on abandoned sites often show little evidence of activity after the fourteenth century, but it is virtually impossible to show that destruction came in 1349 or at some later date. When a tenant died his heir would normally take his place. If, as was possible in 1349, there was no living heir, the lord might add the land to the demesne or join it to an occupied holding or admit an incomer from another settlement. Outlying farmsteads may have been abandoned for better holdings in the main village and landless villagers could have taken the opportunity to better themselves. This process of adjustment may have taken some years. The possible effects of further lesser-known epidemics must also be taken into account. These include no less than five outbreaks of the mysterious 'English Sweat', the last in 1551.

In England as a whole few villages can be shown beyond doubt to have been completely destroyed by pestilence. Among these are Tilgardsley and Tusmore in Oxfordshire, Upton in Gloucestershire and Hale and Elkington in Northamptonshire. Some of these were already weak when plague struck. The only likely case in Norfolk is Little Ringstead. It was quite small, having only 17 payers of Lay Subsidy in 1332, and making a very low contribution in 1334; it was given massive relief from taxation immediately after the Black Death. It seems never to have recovered as it was exempted from the parish tax of 1428 because it had less than ten households. It is absent from the tax list of 1524 and in the eighteenth century there was only a farmhouse there.

Little Ringstead church, 1996. The church is difficult to reach today, standing as it does in the midde of agricultural land. (Poppyland Photos)

Dunston is said to have been depopulated in 1349. According to Blomefield's History of Norfolk most of the parishioners were dead and the land untilled so that the Prioress of Flixton who had the advowson (right to appoint clergy) of the church could not pay the taxes due, presumably because no tithes could be gathered. It had been small to begin with, but it must have recovered as, despite the economic decline of the fourteenth century, it was allowed no reduction of taxation in 1449 and its status in the early sixteenth century compared favourably with parishes nearby. Villages could make good their losses to some extent, especially if their soils yielded well.

Many Norfolk deserted villages, however much they had been weakened by the plague, were still paying taxes a century or more later. Plague, though not an outright destroyer, made many places vulnerable to later happenings. Tudor landlords, when called to account for their depopulating activities, sometimes offered the plague as the reason for the empty sites they themselves had created.

The Actions of Flockmasters

This has been cited as one of the main causes of desertion. The shortage of labour created in the fourteenth century, the attempt to curb rising wages and enforce the manorial duties of villeins by the Statute of Labourers of 1351, and the burden of the Poll Tax, culminated in the Peasants' Revolt of 1381. In Norfolk there is ample evidence of unrest though its exact aims are not entirely clear. The targets of the insurgents seem to have been officials of various kinds and, possibly, the church. It is interesting that some of the villages at which actions took place, Rougham, Palgrave and Kempstone, were subsequently wholly or partly deserted, and that among looted property were flocks of sheep. Perhaps these are early signs of reaction to the first stirrings of a process which was to prove serious in the fifteenth and sixteenth centuries.

To landlords the attractions of turning to sheep farming were now very strong. The price of wool often outstripped the price of grain and large manorial flocks needed comparatively few people to tend them, thus keeping costs low, an advantage if prices for wool were to fall. So began the conversion of arable land to grass which was to see the extinction of many villages in Midland counties and in Yorkshire. Their house platforms, croft boundaries and streets as well as the ridges and furrows of their open fields were long preserved under their grassland covering. The Commissions of Inquiry held in the sixteenth century signified the unease which the movement to pasture caused. What is clear from the evidence the Commissions collected is that, although there were cases of conversion to pasture in Norfolk, they seem to have involved only a few deserted villages. The little hamlet of Holt, near Bawsey, itself deserted, is recorded as being destroyed by conversion to pasture, while Choseley, where 600 acres, including 90 for a park, were enclosed, may also have been a casualty. The usual actions taken by landlords in Norfolk differed from those of their Midland counterparts, but they were effective enough to be a cause of the uprising of 1549, led by Kett.

Sheep had always been an important part of the East Anglian farming economy. Domesday Book shows that sheep were numerous in the western two-thirds of Norfolk and in Broadland, and it contains many references to 'fold-soke' by which tenants' sheep had to be placed in the lord's fold so that his land could be manured. Doubtless medieval farming practice varied from region to region and place to place within the county, but peasants continued to have quite large numbers of sheep and these, together with the lord's flock, manured the arable land. A feature of the system of farming was the foldcourse, an area of land which included open field and heathland and, in some places, meadow land, salt marsh or freshwater fen. Over this area beasts were pastured. In the summer, the animals could not graze on parts under crops but were kept to fallows, commons and heaths. In the winter the stubbles were available for grazing. The flocks of sheep manured or 'tathed' the soil. The foldcourses were controlled by the lord but, in earlier medieval times, when lords were less concerned with flocks, some tenants were allowed to have foldcourses of their own.

After the fourteenth century there were fewer peasants to own sheep, and lords, including monastic houses, began to increase their own flocks. Eventually this increase of the lords' flocks began to infringe the rights of the peasants. Pressure of the extended flocks on the grazing provided by heaths and commons led to overstocking which affected the peasants' grazing rights there. Some lords went further and enclosed commons for their own use. Others enclosed their own arable land to exclude the animals of the peasantry from winter feed. Some landlords extended their own foldcourses over more of the open fields, or set up new ones. All these actions increased landlord profit at the expense of the small peasant cultivator.

Villages which had been weakened by the events of the fourteenth and fifteenth centuries would offer easy targets for landlords wishing to become flockmasters. A large village containing relatively prosperous peasant farmers could stand up to the would-be exploiting landlord much better than a poor shrunken community. Much depended on the attitude of the lord; it was not necessary to depopulate a village to have substantial flocks. The Gawdys of West Harling had large flocks but, as will be shown later, they did not clear the village. However, there are records of some drastic clearances. A man called Thomas Thursby, who was lord of the manor of Gayton, was accused of enclosing commons and wastes in Gayton, Ashwicken, Leziate, Bawsey and Mintlyn. The last three of these are deserted. The accusation also specifically mentioned the destruction of dwellings in the last four of the five places. It was Thursby who had cleared the hamlet of Holt by enclosure.

Of monastic lords, the Cluniac Priory of Thetford, at the Dissolution, was shown to have large flocks of sheep at a number of places. It also held manors at Santon, Lynford and Bodney, three villages which have been deserted. Santon and Lynford each had less than ten households in 1428.

There is evidence to show that sheep were important in the sixteenth century in many surviving villages: Saxthorpe, Little Barningham and Aldborough are examples from north-eastern Norfolk, an area where manors tended to be small. Not all landlords chose or were in a position to become flockmasters on a large scale, while in parts of eastern Norfolk sheep were less important than cattle and much more intensive farming was practised.

A general complaint by the poor of Norfolk in the reign of Elizabeth I concerned oppressive tactics of landlords which were causing villages to decay. Small wonder that rural poverty was on the increase and that people in villages under such attacks moved elsewhere or became beggars.

Engrossment

This is a far less spectacular mode of destruction which took place gradually and unobtrusively. When completed, the former village consisted of no more than a large house and a few farms, with a church serving a tiny congregation. In extreme cases a village might become an estate with a grand house, a home farm and the church, now little more than a family chapel, with a wide scattering of service cottages.

Engrossment was a process by which the lord of the manor might enlarge his demesne by acquiring, by purchase, lands of freehold or copyhold tenants. When a tenant died his heirs might be willing to sell the inheritance instead of seeking admission to the property. It could be undertaken simply to enlarge existing holdings in the village; the land purchased would be added to that of existing tenants so making bigger units which would be more profitable and yield more rent for the lord. On the other hand, additions to the demesne could be made until it covered most of the land in the parish, and so the life of the original village gradually ebbed away.

Engrossment occurred from the sixteenth century onwards and took place against a background of a rapid recovery in the growth of population and a consequent rise in prices. Arable farming was becoming more profitable and favoured the concentration of land in fewer hands.

A recent study of West Raynham by Keith Stride has shown that in the 63 years between 1570 and 1633 no less than 15 tenants, none of them farming more than six acres, were lost to the village. There were also decreases in the number of tenants farming medium-sized holdings, while the demesne increased from just under 25% of the total acreage to just over 65%. In this way the Townshend lords increased their holding in each furlong and even acquired control over some entire furlongs. Some new land was purchased from other manors, thus adding demesne from them or, possibly, evicting copyhold tenants. The result was a drop in the number of tenants farming land against a background of increasing population. The outcome appears to have been migration from the village or an increase in the number of wage-labourers, many of whom must have been employed on the growing Raynham estate. West Raynham survives, although it has lost its church. In a small village such a sequence could have meant the end.

The old open fields were full of intermingled strips which, in the changing order of things, were an obstacle to progressive farming. Lords often sought exchanges of land with surviving tenants or with the church (glebe land) to consolidate their holdings. Along with outright purchases, they are one of the signs of the engrossing process.

Another village where engrossment played a leading part in its decline was Illington. After two manors were united in single ownership in the early sixteenth century, the Gascoyne family, after 1571, began to reduce the settlement by purchasing the rights of copyholders at several times in the reign of Elizabeth I. At the same time, common lands were being taken in. There were still some houses and tenements occupied well into the seventeenth century, but the process continued. The 1664 Hearth Tax recorded only five houses as being chargeable.

Blomefield, writing in the eighteenth century, remarked that Threxton, now deserted, had been reduced to one house in which Mr Knopwood dwelt, occupying 'the whole town which he is said to have lately purchased'. It is not yet clear whether he was the final engrosser or whether he had bought Threxton after others had done it. Purchase of tenements in Narford in the late sixteenth century diminished the village and prepared the way for final dissolution. There are accounts of several other villages, now deserted, where lands had been 'purchased-in' by lords or where the land was completely in the hands of the lord. Further search may bring to light documents which tell the whole story.

In some villages purchasing-in seems to have been associated with a fairly abrupt final stage of desertion. Examples to be examined later are Kilverstone, Hargham, and West Harling. In other, earlier cases, one may hazard a guess that tenants may have been 'persuaded' to sell by the restrictions placed on them by flockmaster lords and that there the two processes were linked.

Emparking

Parks have long been a feature of the English landscape. The first appeared just before the Norman Conquest and their number increased from the twelfth century onwards, when fallow deer were introduced. They were intended to provide meat, especially venison, and wood and timber. They were usually located in the more remote parts of parishes, were rectangular with curved corners or had curving boundaries and were bounded by palisaded banks and ditches. Although many have vanished long since, their outlines can still be traced on maps and aerial photographs, and names such as 'Park Farm' or field names which include 'Park' indicate their position. Examples can be traced in Norfolk in the parishes of Loddon, Old Buckenham and Wymondham.

Warrens, still named on maps, are a reminder of an allied twelfth century introduction to the medieval landscape, the rabbit warren. Also surrounded by banks and ditches, these were created by lords to provide sport and a valuable supply of meat and of furs. Old field names such as Coney Close, Coneygarth, Conynger and Conyfare mark their position, usually on heathland or common grazing in corners of parishes. Often a lodge was built inside the warren. Warren Lodge at Thetford, which once stood in the Prior's Westwick Warren, is a fine surviving example.

Although examples of both medieval features are well known in the Norfolk landscape there is, so far, no evidence to suggest that any settlement was destroyed to make way for either type. However, the landscape park, a later derivative of the medieval form, could be quite different in this respect.

The creation of landscape parks around grand country mansions was a fashion which began to grow in popularity towards the end of the seventeenth century, flourished in the eighteenth and nineteenth centuries and lingered into recent times. Landscape gardeners such as Charles Bridgeman, Lancelot (Capability) Brown, William Kent, Humphrey Repton and others less known, adapted existing features, leaving mature trees and woods but sometimes altering the courses of streams, constructing lakes, ponds and small hills and planting avenues of trees. Old roads were stopped up and replaced by new ones, as many Road Closure Orders show. In some instances, whole villages were removed and new ones were built outside the parks, their churches remaining isolated within, near the great houses. Work begun by one man might be altered or extended by others and plans could be changed at the owner's whim as work progressed.

As David Dymond has shown, the number of Norfolk parks increased over the years. Morden's map of the county (1695) shows some 14, of which a few, like Blickling, Melton Constable, Felbrigg and Kenninghall were already old. Corbridge (1730) showed only 16 on his map but some may have been omitted by either map-maker. Faden's map (1797) showed 117 and by the early twentieth century the Ordnance Survey recorded about 170. They were particularly numerous in the Breckland and in the Goodsand regions. These areas of lighter soils had small villages widely dispersed, allowing space for landowners to indulge their fancies on large estates. There were also more parks near Norwich which, as a source of wealth and social activity, encouraged their creation. Elsewhere, despite increasing numbers, they remained comparatively few and were virtually absent from the low-lying Fens and Broads regions.

Features from the original landscape, such as old field boundaries, often survive in parks, while former roads may appear as hollow ways or are sometimes modified to form driveways. At Wolterton a curving former road has been landscaped by the building of a ha-ha, or low brick wall, to improve the view from the Hall. Earthworks of an old village may still be visible, though sometimes the remains of an abandoned formal garden layout can mislead the unwary, as at Old Hall, West Barsham.

Few villages in Norfolk are known to have been removed and rebuilt. At Holkham the main village was demolished and an existing hamlet extended to replace it. At Houghton, of the old village as shown on a map of about 1720, only the church and an inn remained by 1730. A new village had been begun in 1729 and consisted of ten paired cottages arranged symmetrically on opposite sides of a new street. Since then there have been many alterations to the new village. A comparison between Faden's map and the earliest Ordnance Survey map shows that part of Anmer was removed to allow an extension to the park there. At Letton some surviving buildings around a green were removed when a park was made around the new Letton Hall after 1783. At Wolterton, the Corbridge map of 1732 shows a small community grouped around a rectangular green north of the church; this was subsequently removed when the park was extended. Others are possible examples: at Felbrigg medieval pottery has been found near the isolated church within the park, suggesting removal, but other firmer evidence has yet to be found. On map evidence alone, Haveringland and Westwick may be others of this kind.

Parks may occupy deserted village sites but many were probably made when desertion had long been completed, the empty sites providing opportunities for landscaping. Buckenham Tofts had less than 10 households in 1428 and, having paid less to the 1334 Subsidy than any other village in its hundred, was allowed a 24% reduction on the amount in 1449. It is likely that the village had gone well before the park was made. Much the same was true of Bayfield when its park was laid out in the late eighteenth century. In other cases such as Kilverstone, Narford, Gunton and Hargham, it is not clear whether park-making was part of the original intention or an afterthought.

DATING DESERTION AND IDENTIFYING ITS CAUSE

Although a long list of Norfolk deserted villages can be drawn up, it is rarely easy to pinpoint a date or to single out a cause of destruction. Many villages have few documents to tell their story. Some may have been destroyed or lost, while the whereabouts of others which might exist, is not known. Even when there are plenty of documents they may not give the necessary facts directly but need to be 'read between the lines'. Pottery finds identify sites but they can only be dated within a broad band of years. Even when the general period of desertion is obvious it is not safe to jump to conclusions about the cause. To say that because desertion took place at some time after a certain event, that event was the cause, is unsound.

There are many desertions which are probably not the result of a single cause or not brought about all at once. Much more likely is a slow dwindling or winding down of the settlement caused by different things at various times. Some deserted villages are plain to see, but the straggly or sprawling nature of many Norfolk villages in the first place has helped to make desertion more difficult to recognise and explain.

A PORTRAIT GALLERY OF DESERTION

Unsolved Mysteries: The Desertions of Waterden, Egmere and Quarles

These villages were neighbours and lay in a rough south-to-north line between Little Walsingham and the Creakes. Waterden was in the hundred of Gallow, the others in North Greenhoe.

Waterden lay in a rather damp little valley which may explain its name. According to Domesday Book it had only one lord in 1086, Lambert, who held of Earl Warenne; he also had land in Rudham. In medieval times the manor was held by a succession of families until 1483 when it was sold to the Sefoules, a family which had a good deal of property in north-west Norfolk. It was sold again at the end of the sixteenth century and was bought by Sir Edward Coke of Holkham.

In 1086 Waterden appears to have been small compared with other settlements in its hundred but gave no sign of serious decay. In 1332, 24 persons contributed to the Lay Subsidy; in 1334 Waterden paid a sum which was only thirteenth in order of value out of the eighteen collected from Gallow. Two of the larger sums were joint payments made by two villages, each of which may have contributed less than Waterden's total of £3.4s. Later in the century Waterden had 36 people paying Poll Tax, a little lower than the average for the neighbourhood, but suggesting that it had held its own over some difficult years. This is confirmed by the fact that it was awarded no relief from taxation in the 1350s. It must have avoided the worst of the plague. However, its 1449 Lay Subsidy contribution was reduced by over 31%; six of its immediate neighbours paid totals reduced, on average, by only 19%. Clearly, Waterden had suffered some severe setback in the late fourteenth or early fifteenth centuries. It probably never recovered since it seems not to have been considered as a separate place when the Lay Subsidy of 1524-5 was collected.

A Hall seems to have been built on the site, probably in the sixteenth century and was extensively repaired by Coke in about 1604 or 1605. This is shown with a very few associated buildings on a map of 1714. It was replaced by a new house, with the farm buildings which still survive, in 1781, and they are shown on a map of 1789.

The church of All Saints also survives in mutilated form. The western end, which may have had a tower, is in ruins and a south aisle and chapel have also gone. These must have disappeared before the seventeenth century when the western end and the old aisle were blocked off by walling. A little of the remaining building dates from the thirteenth century. Although a church is mentioned in Domesday, the entry is not clear and it may have been in one of the Creakes.

Aerial photographs reveal crop marks and they and some surviving earthworks show that the small village was grouped around a long narrow green at a meeting of four roads.

All we have about Waterden is this limited framework of information which gives a very rough possible dating for desertion: the reason for the destruction of the community has yet to be found.

Egmere was further up the valley from Waterden and is now marked by three areas of earthworks and the ruins of St Edmund's church, dominated by its spectacular fourteenth century tower.

Egmere church, 1996. The church stands on private land, but it and the churchyard are clearly visible from the road. (Poppyland Photos)

The Bishop held the greater part of Egmere in 1086. It had been a substantial holding but there were signs of decline in population, in cultivation and in valuation. By the fourteenth century Egmere and Quarles were lumped together in contributing to the Lay Subsidy. In 1332 the two settlements had 31 contributors to the tax. In 1334 eight total payments out of 15 in the hundred were higher but Egmere and Quarles together paid quite a large sum. This was not reduced after the Black Death, suggesting that the worst ravages of the outbreak had been escaped. However, Egmere, in 1428, was excused parish tax as there were, by then, less than ten households there. The two settlements were allowed a reduction of 40% in their joint payment to the Lay Subsidy of 1449. Egmere had only a tiny number of contributors to the subsidy in 1524-5.

Apart from these very basic facts there is little more that is yet known. The village seems to have experienced a crime wave in the early fourteenth century. In 1308 three people, one a woman, were charged with the death of Ralph Warde of Egmere. Two were later discharged, but Simon, son of Nicholas of Hanworth, was found guilty but pleaded benefit of clergy. In 1315 a man from Briningham was taken before the Sheriff for the burglary of Egmere church at night; other thieves had apparently escaped.

In the 1550s the decayed village was a target for unscrupulous enterprise. A former parson, together with someone who had leased the rectory, had pulled down part of the church and sent the lead roofing and the largest bell to the coast to be sold overseas. A record later in the century mentions decayed tenements and land in Egmere. In 1602 the church was described as decayed and profaned by the lords and the then incumbent of the living, and it had been made into a barn. A little colour is thus added but we can only conclude that Egmere failed around about 1400 for reasons as yet unknown.

There are some cottages standing near the site of the old manor farm to the south of the church. A hollow way passing the church links it with some earthworks in the valley to the west and can be traced across the intervening ploughed field. The parish boundary with Waterden followed this road; medieval and some late Saxon pottery occurs only on the Egmere side. The earthworks in the valley are of a few tofts on either side of a roadway leading south. This is now followed by a small stream. Some earthworks to the north of the modern road are possibly medieval but have been altered by pit-digging and by the making of ponds.

Quarles is visibly commemorated only by Quarles Farm while OS maps until recently showed the site of a church just to the south. Only a tiny fragment of this remains. The Domesday scribes seem to have had some trouble with the name, writing it as Huerveles and Guervelei. They did not have much to record there as the two parts of the village were outlying farms of Wighton and Creake. Of one it was reported that there was nothing there apart from 60 acres of land, but there could have been a plough team. It is likely therefore that the place was very small and remained so because it was lumped together with Egmere in the 1300s. In the early fourteenth century Quarles figured briefly as a scene of crime. In 1309 Richard the vicar was accused of receiving 18 ells (22.5 yards) of dark blue cloth worth 54 shillings knowing it had been stolen. He was acquitted. In 1313 Clement Estan of Quarles was accused of the death of Parnell, his wife. Some people, lawless or not, were still living there. According to Blomefield, the last parish priest was instituted in 1393. By 1428 there were less than 10 households in Quarles. The church was ruined in 1571 and had already been long in decay. It looks as though a tiny place slowly decayed, but the details have yet to be discovered.

Two Contrasting Shrunken Villages: Rougham and Beachamwell

Rougham is in the west of central Norfolk, about 13km north of Swaffham and 16km to the south-west of Fakenham. The modern village consists of a single street of houses, at the northern end of which lies Rougham Hall. The church of St Mary lies on the western side of the street. From the street, roads extend in several directions to neighbouring places. At first sight it looks a typical small Norfolk village. However, it has already been mentioned in this narrative because of a lost greenside settlement, and there is much more, for Rougham is one of the best examples of a shrunken village in the county. The inhabited area once extended beyond the fork of the roads at the southern end of the street and an additional chapel stood there in medieval times.

To the west of the street lies the remnant of a park laid out by the Hon. Roger North after he purchased the estate in 1691. A fine avenue of lime trees which he planted leads up to the site of the old Hall, demolished later in the eighteenth century. It had been one of the two manor houses of medieval Rougham. North had repaired

SHRUNKEN ROUGHAM

and embellished it; the present Hall had been the domestic annexe of the old one. There is some evidence that this park overlies part of the medieval village.

Beyond the park is an area of grassland in which there are some earthworks. Two diverging hollow ways can be clearly seen. The northern one was known as Massingham Gate or Overgate and led to Great Massingham. ('Gate' here means a street or road, from the Old Norse word 'gata'). Documents tell us that Bradmere Green lay on the northern flank of Massingham Gate and that Green Hall, the second manor house, stood at the south-east corner of this green, near a pool. The southern road was Hildemere Gate or Westgate and led towards King's Lynn, being sometimes known as Lynn Way. Property boundaries are still visible between these roads and to the south of Hildemere Gate, and medieval pottery found occasionally on the surface suggests that these features are medieval. The most

Earthworks at Rougham in February 1984. (D.A. Edwards, Norfolk Air Photography Library, Norfolk Museums Service)

easterly area beyond the junction of the roads and bordering on the park has been disfigured by later pits and by the later development of drainage channels associated with a brickworks. A short length of hollow way suggests that a road from the south led into Hildemere Gate. Foundations of buildings are apparent at some points in the eastern part. Aerial photographs and pottery finds show that inhabited areas once existed along the line of Hildemere Gate as it crosses two further fields, now arable.

The pottery collected from ploughed surfaces ranges in date from the later eleventh century to the late fourteenth or early fifteenth centuries, suggesting that this portion of Rougham was settled soon after the Norman Conquest and abandoned in late medieval times. At the beginning of the fourteenth century the village was prosperous. Only three places in the Launditch hundred contributed more to the subsidy in 1334. In 1449 Rougham's contribution was reduced by over 27%, nearly twice the average for the hundred.

As a cause of such misfortune the Black Death might be suspected; two priests were replaced in Rougham in 1349. Certainly much land changed hands in and immediately after that year suggesting that some were able to benefit from land becoming vacant through mortality. However, some people were still living in the deserted area at the end of the fourteenth century.

A man called John Reed had an interesting part to play in the fortunes of the village. A descendant of villeins, he became lord of the manor of Rougham. A stickler for enforcing his manorial rights, he was also unpopular beyond the confines of Rougham as a collector of the Poll Tax, an assessor of other taxes, a debtor to some people and a harsh creditor to others. Within the village he was attempting to restrict the rights of tenants and to extend and consolidate his own lands. During the Peasants' Revolt of 1381 his house was ransacked and much destruction done by a gang of insurgents who came to the village and were eagerly joined by some of the people of Rougham. The value of his losses was well over £50, a very large sum. When order was restored the guilty got off surprisingly lightly, but some seem to have become noticeably more willing to sell property to, or exchange it, with Reed. There is some evidence to suggest that such arrangements led to movement out of the western end of the village, and this must have been of some advantage to Reed. It is possible that nature was partly on his side. The onset of wetter conditions may have made life difficult in western Rougham in the early fifteenth century, as people began to be fined for not maintaining ditches and causing floods. Having a flock of his own, Reed, through the manor court, was restricting the movement of tenants' sheep, and it seems that his activities were all focused on the need to make his enterprise more profitable.

Reed's heiress daughter married a Yelverton and the estate was held by their descendants until the last, Yelverton Peyton, sold to Roger North. What Reed began the Yelvertons certainly finished.

In 1511 an agreement made between a Yelverton lord and the Priory of Castle Acre, letting part of his manor, describes as shack or seasonal pasture the area which includes the earthworks, confirming thus that it had long been abandoned. The agreement, while safeguarding the rights of tenants, laid down that the number of sheep to be kept was 19 hundreds. Yelverton retained the right of free access to the warren to 'cherysh his conyes'. In the Inquisition of 1517 Yelverton was cited for having converted 200 acres of arable to sheep pasture.

By the time Roger North bought the estate the village had undergone further decay. He began a history of Rougham and described the remains of farms and dwellings, the signs of neglect and of damage by fire. He mentioned that purchasing-in had left only a cluster of houses around the church. He spent heavily on repairs and restoration and probably saved the village from extinction.

It is interesting that Rougham should have been one of a number of places singled out for attack in 1381 and that the reason for the particular attention of the mob was the presence there of an oppressive sheep-farming lord. Archaeological evidence points to the late fourteenth century for the beginning of change in Rougham. Whether Reed caused this change or simply took the opportunities opened to him in a weakening village is uncertain. It is fortunate that an unusually full store of documents allows us to piece together so much of the story.

Beachamwell is a large parish lying some 8km to the south-west of Swaffham. Until recently part of its western boundary followed the Dark Age earthwork known variously as Bicham Ditch or the Devil's Dyke (easy to confuse with similar features of that name elsewhere in East Anglia). Although not strictly within Breckland, much of the northern part of the parish has sandy soils which are reminiscent of that region. The settlement is concentrated in the southern portion below 15m Ordnance Datum in between the valleys of two very small streams which drain south-westwards to join the Wissey.

The west end of All Saints church, Beachamwell, was still standing in 1989 but collapsed in July of that year. (D A Edwards, Norfolk Air Photographs Library, Norfolk Museums Service..)

In Beachamwell the signs of shrinkage are obvious. The present village is grouped neatly around a little open space near the church of St Mary which contains work of pre- or immediate post-Conquest date. Some of the nearby houses are of the early nineteenth century. Beachamwell Hall was rebuilt in 1906 after a fire and stands apart in a small park. The outbuildings are of late eighteenth century date. There are, in addition, two ruined churches: St John's is to the west of the village and has the remains of a moat near it, All Saints' is quite far away to the south with some earthworks and the soil markings of a large moat nearby. A map of 1776 shows the village grouped in somewhat less orderly fashion around St Mary's with a few buildings near All Saints'.

It has been suggested frequently that Beachamwell was once two villages, Bicham and Well. Well is said to have been the part by All Saints'. Certainly, Domesday Book records 'Well' separately from 'Bicham'. In 1254 an ecclesiastical parish tax list gives three names, Bechamwell, Bicham St Mary and Parva Bicham, obviously corresponding to the parishes served by the three churches. Later evidence shows that Parva Bicham was St John's. In fact the medieval village seems to have been considered one place in which there were three localities holding the name Becham in common.

In 1334 Beachamwell was named as one place and was one of only 60 places in the county taxed at £10 or more. It paid the seventh highest contribution in the hundred of Clackclose. The reduction of taxation allowed for it in 1449 was one of the three lowest in Clackclose and its contribution was the fifth highest in the hundred. It was thus prosperous and maintained that prosperity in the teeth of the general misfortunes of the fourteenth century.

Surveys made have suggested a large settlement at this time. The earthworks near All Saints' church include a hollow way apparently leading south towards the neighbouring village of Caldecote, also long deserted. To the west of it, the church ruins, some of which can be dated to the twelfth century, lie within a distinct churchyard, and there are some platforms and an enclosure on either side of it. To the east of the hollow way are several more enclosures. From the whole area of the earthworks some Late Saxon and much more medieval pottery has been collected. Some Romano-British pottery has also been found. On arable land to the west and south-west much more pottery of the same types has occurred with the addition of sherds of Middle Saxon date and some prehistoric pieces. On and around the large moated feature under cultivation some distance to the east of the church quantities of medieval pottery have been found, suggesting a manorial site of that period. In land beside the track leading north to the present village some Late Saxon and much medieval pottery occurs, and a few pieces of prehistoric pottery have also been found. It appears on this evidence that settlement was well established in this part of the village by Late Saxon times at least, and possibly earlier. It intensified in medieval times and almost certainly joined with the part around St Mary's. When the ruins of All Saint's collapsed in 1989 part of a Late Saxon wheel-headed cross was found in the rubble, giving additional evidence of pre-medieval activity here.

Just to the west of St Mary's church and to the south of the road finds of Early, Middle and Late Saxon date have been made among much medieval material.

Between the ruins of St John's church and the road to the east a similar range of finds has been made. Middle Saxon pottery occurs close to the church which stands on a roughly circular mound. However, none of the existing church fabric appears older than the fourteenth century.

There is thus evidence of fairly early activity in the vicinity of each of the churches. By medieval times they lay within a more or less continuous area of settlement which was roughly crescentic in shape. This matches the impression of well-being given by the level of subsidy payments up to 1449. None of the parishes was exempted from the parish tax of 1428.

There were three medieval manors, one of them being that of Well Hall near All Saints'. The moat near St John's can be equated with one of the others - Ashfield's or Cherville's. It has been suggested that amalgamation of these manors may have caused the contraction of the village. Two of them had been acquired by one family about 1500, but the third was not added by purchase until 1760, long after decay had set in.

The neighbourhood of All Saints' was virtually abandoned by 1721 when the church was said to have been in ruins for 33 years and the inhabitants of its parish too few to afford its repair. It had been maintained by the Athow lords of Well Hall as a family burial place for years before that; their arms, with the date 1612, were placed on the west wall (now fallen). St John's church seems to have been disused by the mid-sixteenth century and was probably abandoned at the Reformation. Blomefield records that poor people had built little cottages on the site in the eighteenth century implying that the area had been empty for some time previously. Only a small portion of the church was standing by then.

The decay of Beachamwell must have occurred at some time after 1450 and was well advanced by the seventeenth century. Unfortunately, documents covering this period have so far not come to hand. The only pointers to a more exact timing of desertion are to be found in wills left by Beachamwell people. Many give requests for burial or make some other reference to their parish church. Of 11 dating from before 1500, six mention St Mary's, four All Saints', and only one St John's. Of 48 from between 1500 and 1600, eight, distributed evenly over the century, name All Saints', one named St John's, five made no specific reference and 34 named St Mary's. St John's was not mentioned after 1541, when the parson of St Mary's left a short gown to the parson there. St John's, unlike the other two, was omitted from an inventory of church goods made in 1552. By 1603 Beachamwell had an estimated population of about 370. In 1664, 35 heads of household were charged for a total of 79 hearths (Sir Christopher Athow had 21 of them). How many poor people were excused from the tax is not known.

On this slender evidence it seems likely that Beachamwell had declined to a settlement concentrated about St Mary's by the middle of the sixteenth century. In the absence of fuller information we cannot point to any special cause.

Some Victims of Flockmasters: Thorpland, Alethorpe, Pudding Norton and Sturston

Thorpland lay in a north-eastern salient of the parish of Fakenham. The only evidence of its former existence on the map is the presence of Thorpland Hall with Thorpland Lodge nearby.

Like its large neighbour it was in the hundred of Gallow and is mentioned in Domesday as an outlying farm or berewick of Fakenham, the centre of an estate which had belonged to King Harold. This royal estate included other places in the area. Thorpland had one carucate (120 acres) of land, one plough-team and a recorded population of one serf. The subordinate nature of this small place is reflected in 1316 when it was shown as part of Fakenham and in medieval subsidy lists when it was lumped together with that place. In the 1334 Subsidy listing it was not mentioned at all.

According to Blomefield, 90 people lived in this hamlet at the time of Edward I and it had its own chapel of St Thomas (presumably Becket), though baptisms and burials could only take place at the mother church of Fakenham, where there was also a chapel of St Thomas the Martyr.

It seems quite likely that Thorpland may have increased in size during the medieval period. As late as 1496, after population in the county as a whole had declined, a list of tenants paying rent shows that there were 26 in Thorpland, assuming that all were living in the hamlet. The chapel is mentioned in a few fifteenth century wills: while one of 1419 mentions that it had a cemetery by that time, another of 1492 records a small bequest for repairs. There was also a Gild of St Thomas at Thorpland. A gild of this kind was a group of

DESERTED VILLAGES NEAR FAKENHAM

men and women who had formed an association for mutual spiritual advantage. It paid for prayers and masses for the bodily welfare of its members and for their souls in Purgatory. Its existence in Thorpland is some indication of an active, though small community.

Thorpland was taxed separately in 1524-5 when a very small total was collected from a handful of inhabitants, an entry very like those for neighbouring deserted villages. Not everyone would have appeared on such lists, only those above a certain level of wealth.

It seems likely that the end for Thorpland came not long after this. In 1520, in the Court of Star Chamber, tenants of the lordship of Fakenham brought a series of complaints against Henry Fermor. They included allegations that he had purchased lands there, including a foldcourse for 300 sheep, and inclosed them and stopped common ways, all at Thorpland, and had also destroyed houses. He was said to have established, over 13 years before, in Thorpland and Fakenham, a foldcourse of 1000 ewes, pasturing them on lands which were, in reality, fields and common of Fakenham to the extent of 100 acres, worth more in value than 200 acres of pasture within those towns. He had also pastured 800 sheep within a foldcourse in the neighbouring fields of Sculthorpe, despite the fact that he owned only five acres in that town. He was accused of impounding tenants' cattle and of letting houses to poor men without the land which should have been attached, thus encouraging them to exert rights which were not theirs. The Jury found the substance of the allegations true, confirming that Fermor either barred tenants' own sheep from pastures, or charged them 4d for grazing. All this is characteristic behaviour of an oppressive landlord. The Commission of Inquiry of 1517 noted that Fermor had enclosed lands elsewhere in Tittleshall, Hindringham and Erpingham (100 acres).

Henry Fermor had been a rich merchant of London who gained a foothold in the county by marriage. He built the fine manor house at East Barsham just to the north of Fakenham and became one of the greatest flockmasters in England, having more than 15,000 sheep in 20 flocks in 1521.

By 1611 the chapel of St Thomas had become a barn and was granted by the Crown to two London gentlemen who promptly conveyed it to a third person. In 1632 it was still being used as a barn and was leased with a neighbouring cottage. The chapel is now no more than a fragment of a ruin just to the south-east of Thorpland Hall which has been described, by Pevsner, as one of the finest pieces of sixteenth century brick architecture in Norfolk. It appears to have been built on the site of what had never been a large place and one which fell easy victim to an ambitious lord.

Alethorpe lay a little further to the south-east of Thorpland; the site now lies within a salient of the parish of Little Snoring. Unlike Thorpland, it was once a separate parish. This was also a Domesday berewick of Fakenham, part of the royal estate. It seems to have been slightly more significant than Thorpland, having one carucate of land, three bordars and a serf, one plough-team on the demesne and two oxen among the men, and two acres of meadow.

In 1316 it was recorded as still being part of the Fakenham lordship though it was grouped with Pensthorpe. Unlike Thorpland, it was listed separately in Lay Subsidy lists. In 1329 10 people contributed to this tax, in 1332, 11. These would have been heads of households suggesting, perhaps, a population of 50 or 60, not including any households too poor to contribute to the tax. According to Blomefield there had been 30 houses in the time of Edward I (1272-1307) and baptisms and burials were permitted at the church or chapel of All Saints'. It was still standing in 1419.

It was taxed separately in 1334, the total assessed being the lowest in the hundred - even lower than that for Pensthorpe, its near and now deserted neighbour. It was allowed no relief after the Black Death and no relief in 1449; it had 12 payers of Poll Tax in 1379. All these facts point to little decline. Its nearest neighbours were allowed, on average, reductions of 19% in 1449. A rental of 1496 lists 10 rent payers in Alethorpe. The contribution the village made to the 1524-5 subsidy compares well with those made by several villages still existing today, though as the number paying was small it points to the affluence of a few.

The end for Alethorpe came later in the sixteenth century. A number of the inhabitants complained to the Sheriff of Norfolk, Nathaniel Bacon, about the activities of William Dye or Day. They claimed that he had broken up their enclosed lands to allow free passage for his sheep, that he had driven his sheep over their newly sown winter corn and into their yards and orchards 'for that he knoweth that wee... want ability to contend with him at the common law', and that he had encouraged his sons and his servants to beat and abuse his neighbours 'affirming openly in threatening and menacing sort, that he shall and will breake our hart stringes'. He had also overstocked the tenants' small commons so that their beasts were starved of feed. He had enclosed his own land preventing tenants' animals from grazing there after harvest but turned his own enlarged flock into the stubbles of the remaining open fields. Dye also removed fences from his yards so purposely allowing villagers' beasts to stray there and then the animals 'are so hunted and beaten, bayted and otherwise abused as is incredible that any Christian should offer the like unto dum beasts and intolerable for us to endure'.

Witnesses gave evidence before Nathaniel Bacon and other Commissioners of the Duchy of Lancaster on two occasions in 1580, one at Fakenham, one at Little Walsingham. Various statements made included frequent testimonies about a particular croft of 30 acres in the South Field of Alethorpe. Parts of this had been enclosed over a number of years by different tenants, including the plaintiff Thomas Langdon. The dispute between Langdon and Dye had come to a head because he had prevented Dye and his shepherd from feeding sheep on the croft. He had even taken Dye's sheep off the croft and placed them in the Queen's pound at Fakenham. Some witnesses deposed that the custom of the manor had long allowed tenants to enclose lands 'at will and pleasure' and keep them several (separated) without any punishment or disturbance. Others testified that Dye had been duly seized of his father's messuage (a William Dey was a rent-payer in 1496) and that he was the only person with foldcourse rights in Alethorpe. This foldcourse extended from Alethorpe village to Pensthorpe in the south, touched on Fakenham in the west and upon Thorpland to the north - virtually the entire parish. One witness said that Sir William Fermor was likewise an owner and had not challenged Dye's right to pasture sheep on the 30 acre croft. Dye may have been leasing land from the Fermors or he may have been their tenant. The position is not clear, nor is the outcome of the Commissioners' investigations. It seems likely that Dye defended himself successfully against Langdon and the other tenants who were doubtless behind him because by the end of the century there was no need for a church; in 1602 it was decayed and was used as a barn. Today only Alethorpe Hall marks the site of the village on maps.

Pudding Norton lay a short distance to the south of Fakenham. Apart from Norton Hall and the remains of the church shown on maps, this is one of the finest groups of earthworks remaining in Norfolk.

The village stood on a gentle slope extending eastwards to a small stream flowing north to join the Wensum at Fakenham. It lay on either side of a street which ran south from the present Hall. Near the southern end of the field in which the earthworks lie the street forked in two, with one branch continuing south, the other turning east. Beyond the Hall the street continued northwards in the direction of the mill at Fakenham. It is likely that the village may have extended beyond the limits of the field.

Long straight banks extending back on either side of the street mark toft boundaries. Within the tofts a few faint raised features may have been buildings and the hollows, yards. The tofts nearest the site of the church of St Margaret are irregular in shape and may date from earlier days. The more distant ones are larger and more

Earthworks at Pudding Norton. (Cambridge University Collection of Air Photographs)

uniform. They could be a sign of later, planned expansion. In all, there are 22 tofts, 13 of them to the east of the street. South of the churchyard is a short length of hollow way marking a former lane. To the east of the road, a little further north, another hollow way opens out into what may have been common pasture. There are two small linked moat-like features east of the Hall. The remains of the church date almost entirely from the twelfth century.

Pudding Norton was another outlying part of the Fakenham estate. In 1086 it had 60 acres of land, one bordar, half a plough team, half an acre of meadow, one runcey or cob and one pig. There were also seven sokemen (free men under certain obligations) with 20 acres and one plough-team. It had a church with eight acres valued at 6d. Like Alethorpe and Thorpland it was certainly not large. Unfortunately, very little documentary information has survived from medieval times. In 1329, 15 heads of households paid the Lay Subsidy, suggesting a total population of at least 70. The village's contribution to the 1334 tax was the lowest in the whole hundred of Brothercross but it had no reduction after the Black Death or in 1449 and, as it had more than 10 households, it was not exempt from the parish tax in 1428. These bare facts allow us to assume that, though small, it was stable. A few fifteenth century wills show money being given to two gilds - of St Margaret and St Katherine - and there were bequests to the church.

The rolls of the Lay Subsidy of 1524-5 show a small number of people paying total sums which compare quite well with places still in existence. A Subsidy roll of 1543 is revealing. Out of a sum of £9 1s 2d, Sir William Fermor paid £8 for land and Alyce Perne, a widow, 20s for goods. The remainder was contributed by four people. Fermor was the son of Henry Fermor, encountered in the story of Thorpland, and lived, not at Pudding Norton, but in East Barsham. Like his father, he was a flockmaster. Obviously he must have had extensive interests in the village in 1543 and it is worth noting that he presented clergy to the living in 1537 and again in 1549. After the Dissolution the site of the Hempton Priory of Augustinian Canons was granted in 1545 to Fermor, and with it went Hempton Priory manor which extended into Pudding Norton, thus increasing his control of the village. In his will of 1557 he left 20s for the repair of the church and 11d to every house in the village. His nephew sold the family interests when he inherited. However, it seems likely that William Fermor had behaved as his father had done elsewhere in the lordship of Fakenham. If so, it appears that his successors did nothing to preserve the village as, by 1602, the church had been long decayed and it was not known who had been responsible for its destruction. The new lords, however, were Catholic recusants and this may be, in part, an explanation. When Blomefield's History of Norfolk was compiled in the eighteenth century, Pudding Norton was described as a depopulated village with only a hall or manor house and a farmhouse remaining. A part of the small square church tower was then standing, much as it is today.

Sturston was in the heart of the Norfolk Breckland, commonly seen, with its light sandy soils, as a harsh setting for settlement. This is a distinct contrast to Rougham, Quarles, Egmere and Waterden whose sites lie in the Goodsand region and the Fakenham group located in the upper Wensum valley.

Sturston lay on the southern side of a small stream flowing west to join the Wissey. With the stream forming its northern boundary, the parish extended southwards on to the higher and drier Breck landscape. This is typical of the layout of a Breckland parish. It is worth noting here that, although the populations of the parishes of medieval Breckland may have been less numerous than those in surrounding areas, recent work by Mark Bailey has shown that they were much more prosperous than has been thought.

In 1086 Sturston was, apart from two very small holdings, in the hands of Lovell whose overlord was Ralph Baynard. He also held land from Baynard in West Dereham. In Sturston he held six carucates (720 acres) of land and a further 10 acres of meadow. There were also 16 freemen attached to the demesne who held 241 acres. The two small holdings accounted for another 90 acres. The total recorded population in 1086 was 22; it had been 29 in 1066. There were other apparent signs of decline over the 20 years. The number of plough-teams among the freemen had fallen from six to three and the number among the men on the demesne had fallen from three teams to two oxen. The number of teams on the demesne could have been increased from two to three. All this seems to point to quite a lot of land not being under the plough. One important change was that the number of sheep had risen to 200. Breckland was, in 1086, already an area where sheep were very important and by the later thirteenth century parishes were carrying large numbers, many of them belonging to tenants. A further medieval development in Sturston was the creation of a rabbit warren.

To the Lay Subsidy of 1332, 19 heads of Sturston households contributed. In 1334 the village paid a total which was only thirteenth in size out of 16 for the hundred, but still quite comparable with several other parishes in central Breckland. No reduction was allowed after the Black Death and the Poll Tax was levied on 19 people. It would seem that the strength of the community remained much the same despite the difficulties of the century. However, although it was not exempt from the parish tax of 1428, it was allowed a reduction of over 25% on the 1449 Lay Subsidy, one of the largest in the hundred. A closer look at some of these figures is revealing, despite their questionable reliability. Sturston's 1334 payment was only 55% of the average payment made by its six neighbours; the number of its Poll Tax payers was only 69% of the average number of theirs, and their average reduction in 1449 was only 15%. Sturston must have been comparatively small and had been more seriously hurt in the fifteenth century.

During the reign of Henry I, Sturston had passed to the Clare or Fitzwalter family and they had divided it between two sub-tenants. It was not united again until the sixteenth century when it was in the hands of the Shacklock family. By this time the village had probably declined still further as it had the smallest number of persons contributing what was the smallest total in Grimshoe Hundred to the Subsidy of 1524-5. From the Shacklocks, Sturston passed to a member of the Jermyn family from Rushbrook in Suffolk. It was Edmund Jermyn, as Keith Allison has pointed out, who must have decided to remove the small village.

In 1597 he was accused of trying to take the glebe land, which consisted of some 400 acres of arable, and a foldcourse, for 500 sheep. Land belonging to institutions such as the church was often the last to remain untouched by a grasping lord, surviving in scattered pieces embedded here and there within his swollen estate. This seems true of Sturston. Jermyn's accusers said that he had pulled down all the houses apart from the parsonage, destroyed ancient boundaries by ploughing, made new ditches and taken all the commons for himself. The witnesses called at an Inquiry gave varying accounts which outlined the final days of the village. One had known Sturston when there were eight houses, three had lived there when there were six, and a man, by then living in Tottington just to the east, said there were five inhabited houses when he lived in Sturston. In 1597 four were still standing but Jermyn was using one for malting, one for brewing and one as a dairy. The fourth was falling into decay. The witnesses said that part of the Sturston heathland, formerly common land, had been enclosed. The boundaries of the glebe had become so uncertain because of the changes which had come to the village that orders were given to survey them and the judgement was given against Jermyn.

One interesting point about this case is that it gives us some idea of what happened to displaced villagers. Apart from the man in Tottington, witnesses from Thompson, Stow Bedon and Little Wretham, nearby, the last being itself deserted now, and Saham Toney and Tittleshall, much further away, all said that they had formerly lived in Sturston.

According to Blomefield, writing before 1739, the manor house was the only dwelling left. The church of Holy Cross was still standing just to the south of the manor. He described it as a small building of flint, 26 feet long and 14 feet wide, with a tiled roof. The chancel was gone, the foundations only remaining, while the western tower, low, square and of flint, was ruinous and open from top to bottom. It was served by a curate on a very low stipend. The living, before the Reformation, had been well endowed and had belonged to the Priory of Dunmow, which had had a rectory house there.

Nearly 300 years after its disappearance, White's Directory for 1845 reveals a shadowy existence for Sturston which is typical of the way in which memories of a deserted village often linger on. In that year Sturston had a population of 47. There were 1802 acres of 'sandy land' in one farm, belonging to Lord Walsingham. Apart from the farm there was a 'prolific' rabbit warren of some 800 acres. The church was a heap of ruins and had been so for a long time, though the burial ground was still occasionally used. According to the parish registers of Tottington it was regarded as an extra-parochial place.

The few inhabitants appear to have attended church at Tottington or at Stanford.

By the 1930s the population was in the twenties. Early twentieth century maps show 'Sturston Hall' as an antiquity, Sturston Warren, Sturston Carr, and Sturston as a parish name. Sturston has been in a military training area emptied of people since 1942. All that remains are a few remnants of the Hall, apparently seventeenth century, the rectangular foundations of the church tower and some medieval earthworks, including a nearby moat. On the most recent maps the moat, the carr and the warren are all that are shown.

Some Later Casualties: Kilverstone, Hargham and West Harling

Kilverstone, near Thetford, was owned by the Wrights, a family of flockmasters, in the late sixteenth century. The medieval village lay on the north bank of the Thet and the parish stretched across the heathland to Ringmere, the focus of five parishes. A small village, slightly less prosperous than its neighbours, it survived the middle ages. Its two manors had been granted to monasteries - Monkshall to Thetford Priory and Coxford to Coxford Priory in East Rudham. After the Dissolution they eventually came into the single ownership of the Cornwallis family, one of whom sold to Thomas Wright in 1588.

Wright was immediately involved in legal action over the commons, a case inherited from Charles Cornwallis. A man called John Stalham claimed to be a tenant of the Crown with rights of common and alleged that Wright had been ploughing-up commons, enlarging his flocks and blocking a road. The dispute ended in a Court of Exchequer Inquiry in 1593 and it appears that Wright defended himself successfully. Subsequent actions in 1619 showed that Stalham's claims were quite fraudulent. The living of Kilverstone had been held by Butley Priory in Suffolk before the Reformation. Stalham had gone to London and claimed that the parsonage, after the Dissolution, must have become Crown property. He had obtained a lease of the property. In 1585 he had ejected the parson, who was too old to resist and, after installing himself, claimed foldcourse rights. In 1619, a new parson, backed by leading parishioners, brought the Stalham family to court. They, pending the outcome, were forbidden to ransack the property any further.

As early as 1593 Wright had taken three tenements in hand, and between 1596 and 1621 he and his family were purchasing more lands and messuages. Some of these were bought from heirs who lived in other villages and even as far away as Gloucestershire. These happenings do not appear to have caused any immediate decline in population. Lists of Rates levied as late as the 1650s show that there were still members of old Kilverstone families present in some numbers while Overseers' Accounts a little later show that there were also present people too poor to rate.

The Wrights were very prosperous, with other flocks in Croxton, Weeting and Carbrooke. The second member of the family to hold Kilverstone built a new manor house to replace the two medieval ones; parts of it are incorporated in the present Hall.

The village finally dwindled away in the late seventeenth century. Old family names had begun to disappear by the time the 1672 Hearth Tax list was compiled and Blomefield, in 1737, said that all tenancies had been purchased-in and only eight houses remained. Quiet but steady engrossment had created an estate.

An aerial photograph of 1946 shows an area of earthworks well to the south-east of the church, but most of these have since gone. Pottery from that site is of the thirteenth and fourteenth centuries, suggesting that it represents a medieval extension of the village or a movement away from a position nearer the church. The round-towered church has been much restored but still includes substantial twelfth century work. The medieval manor houses stood to the south of the church, on either side of a lane. Romano-British pottery occurring with the medieval material indicates activity of that period somewhere in the vicinity.

Hargham lay just to the south of Attleborough on the margins of the clay lands of central Norfolk and the sands of Breckland. Throughout the Middle Ages it remained a tiny village of only modest prosperity, but holding its own by comparison with neighbours. The sole incident of note before the seventeenth century seems to have been a dispute between Henry Gurney, lord of Hargham, and John Lant of Beck Hall in Wilby, which was over common rights and which lasted from 1595 to 1597. Although Lant received the verdict doubts seem to have lingered into the late seventeenth century.

HARGHAM in 1629

(after W. Hayward)

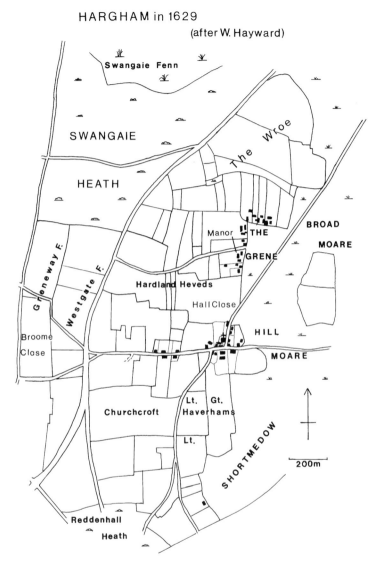

Two surveys of Hargham exist, one with a map dated 1629 and an updated version accompanied by maps in a field book of 1681. The maps show a small village distributed along the western edge of a common, with one cluster of houses near the church and another near the site of the present Hall. The manor house stood near the site of the modern Hall Farm.

Changes in the fabric of village life seem to have begun with some enclosure from commons, and manorial restrictions there are recorded between 1640 and 1660. Annotations in the field book and other evidence show that Nicholas Hare, lord of Hargham, was purchasing-in lands and houses from tenants, particularly at the north end of the village, in the 1680s. By 1709 the clearance was probably complete as an agreement made in 1708 between Ralph Hare and Humphrey Yallop of Wilby shows that Yallop received certain lands, including yards and crofts, but that Hare retained rights to remove materials from 'the lately demolished houses'. In 1753 the church bells were sold to repair the church as the parishioners were too few to afford it and the roof and parts of the walls were down. The church, with a ruined tower and most of the nave gone, remains. Ironically, the nave was the portion of a church assigned to lay people of whom there were by then almost none. The parson then was a relative of the lord of the manor. The Hall, of the late seventeenth century, lies in a small park. A moat, relic of a medieval manorial site, lies in a small wood south-east of the church. There is no obvious motive for the clearance except estate building.

West Harling, in the Thet valley in eastern Breckland, was deserted in the first half of the eighteenth century. Although it had been held for a long time by the Gawdy family, who were flockmasters, they were not responsible for its end.

The village was originally part of a cluster of settlements all named 'Herlinga' in 1086. By medieval times, three of these had become known as West Harling, with its church of All Saints', Middle Harling, with St Andrew's church, and, at the western end, Harling Thorpe, the site of Seckford (or Hackford) manor. Middle Harling had been active from Middle Saxon times as finds of pottery, coins and metalwork have shown. From 1066 onwards it seems to have declined. Its church was demolished in 1543 and it was added to West Harling. By the early sixteenth century a member of the numerous Gawdy family acquired the manors of West and Middle Harling through marriage and, in 1564, purchased Seckford as well.

MEDIEVAL WEST HARLING

/// Medieval Sites

O   Site of West Harling Hall

::::   18C Park

1 Km

Apart from the obvious decline of Middle Harling to a subordinate hamlet, the medieval period was successfully weathered. Although the settlements had lost some ground by the fifteenth century, they remained comparable with others in Breckland. As well as the main cluster around All Saints' church there were outlying street-type hamlets at Harling Thorpe and Storkisey, probably near Stonehouse Farm.

The Gawdys had large flocks of sheep; in 1655 there were three, totalling 1585, in 1665 there were 3112 in five flocks. However, there seems to have been no evidence of decline in the settlement during this time; the names of various streets, Churchgate, Thursmore, Storkisey and Thorpe, appear in records into the early eighteenth century. The Gawdys were, however, less prosperous. Profits from sheep fell in the seventeenth century and wealth had been squandered in the pursuit of offices in County and in Parliament. Sir John Gawdy was deaf and incapable of speech and was thus at a grave disadvantage in business. Sir Bassingbourn Gawdy died, accidentally, in 1723 without male heirs. The property was sold to Joshua Draper who, in 1731, sold again to Richard Gipps.

Draper began the changes. He demolished the moated Berdewell Hall, home of medieval lords, and began purchasing-in. Gipps undertook a whole series of such actions so that, by 1738, apart from the parsonage, there were just Harling House, a blacksmith's shop and three farms - at Thorpe, at Middle Harling and at Stonehouse. A southern aisle of the church was demolished because there were so few parishioners. In 1743 a new rectory was built at a discreet distance from Gipps' new Hall, the old one near the church having been removed. A proposal made in 1737 to demolish the chancel, not carried out, was backed by a statement, supported by Gipps himself, that he had bought all the houses, apart from one small cottage, and so had reduced the number of dwellings.

Although the Gawdys had a deer park and had made some enclosures, Gipps' heirs, William Croftes and his son Richard, carried through much more drastic changes, closing an old road and making a new one, and laying out a park. William even uprooted the foundations of Middle Harling church to build up marshy ground.

Today, the church stands virtually alone. The remains of two moats are nearby and there are some good earthworks at Thorpe, together with a fragment of what may have been a watermill. In the church is a bust of Richard Gipps by Joseph Wilton, placed there by his great-nephew, Richard Croftes. The Hall Gipps built was demolished in 1931 and conifer plantations cover much of his estate.

A Case of Gentle Evolution

Letton Hall lies in a small park near Shipdham, some 7.5km north-east of Watton in mid-Norfolk where there are heavier soils. It was once the site of a medieval village first mentioned in Domesday Book. The earliest versions of its name include Lecton (1200); this may refer to the small stream (Old English 'lece', meaning 'brook') which flows through Letton to join the Yare. Alternatively, it might

LETTON in c.1750

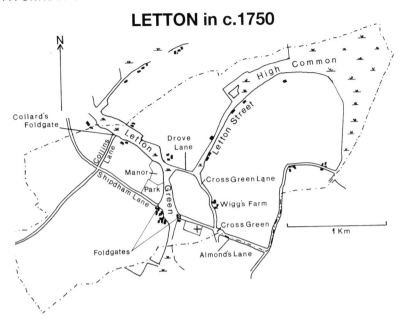

mean 'leek farm' (Old English 'leac-tun').From the evidence of Domesday and later tax payments, Letton was probably a small place. It may have had a population of somewhere above 100 in the twelfth and thirteenth centuries. It had a church which was recorded in 1086. By the mid-fifteenth century there had been some decline, Letton having a much greater reduction of taxation in 1449 than its near neighbours.

In the twelfth century the major holding in Letton was split. One part remained in lay hands, the other, together with the advowson (right to present clergy) of the church was granted to the Cluniac Priory of Lewes in Sussex which retained it until the Dissolution. The village probably had a watermill and, just possibly, a windmill, and there is enough evidence from the fourteenth century to show that there were some houses facing westwards onto a common. Sheep were important in the economy: the wealthiest contributor to the Poll Tax was invoking the Statute of Labourers against his shepherd. There may have been some discontent in Letton as a man living there was indicted for his misdemeanours in the Peasants' Revolt (1381).

In the early 1500s Letton was still a small but active community which included a metal worker and a weaver, though some seem to have had property elsewhere. An agreement between the Brampton lord of Letton and Richard Southwell of Woodrising shows that each had flocks of sheep, together totalling 600, in Letton and describes Letton Green as extending right across the parish and linking with commons in Cranworth and Shipdham. Brampton undertook not to enclose any more land without permission. Soon after 1546 Letton church was abandoned, the living being consolidated with Cranworth.

A survey of 1627 suggests that Letton had become a community of scattered farms, many of them on the margins of the green, on the southern side of which was the manor house. It also shows that much land was enclosed, although the green survived and was to do so until 1783. Seventeenth century rent lists show a gradual decline from eleven persons in 1622 to six in 1687. However, the Hearth Tax of 1666 listed 21 households (with 59 hearths, 18 in the manor house) and there were also six poor people and two poor-houses.

Eighteenth century Poor Rate Lists show a steady decline from 22 parishioners in 1748-9 to 12 in 1778-9. Soon after, in 1783, orders were made to divert certain roads to prepare for a park. This was to be the setting for a new mansion to replace the old manor house, the seat of Brampton Gurdon Dillingham. Designed by Sir John Soane, this was built near the old manor house in 1786-8.

Earthworks of part of the medieval village remained in the park until 1978. The foundations of the church survive in woodland and there are traces of a hollow way leading past it.

A Classic Emparking

Holkham Hall within its extensive park is a prominent feature of the Norfolk landscape. The village lies outside the park on the coastal road while New Holkham, formerly called Longlands Village, built in 1793-5, is at the southern entrance.

Medieval Holkham was quite a thriving place. In the fourteenth century, as in other coastal settlements, its lay inhabitants contributed substantially to subsidies, while a number of monastic houses had lucrative holdings. In 1267 one of its lords had obtained the grant of a market there. There was decline by the fifteenth century but it was not excessive by comparison with neighbouring places. In 1517 evidence was given that 130 acres had been converted to pasture and various decayed tenements totalling 200 acres were mentioned as being consolidated. The village must have contracted to some extent.

Holkham Hall and its extensive park. Earthworks from the village are still visible in the foreground of the photograph. (Derek A Edwards, Norfolk Air Photographs Collection, Norfolk Museum Service)

Fortunately, a map of 1590 shows us old Holkham. It consisted of two settlements: the main village grouped around a small common on either side of which stood manor houses, and a small coastal cluster called 'The Stathe', known to have existed by the fourteenth century at least. The common was the site of the market place. The church had been standing in isolation to the north-west of the main village since medieval times at least.

The two manors eventually passed into the hands of the Coke family in 1572. The easternmost manor house was sited where the Hall and garden now stand.

The creation of the park began in 1722 and the lake was made by damming a small stream. Demolition of houses began in 1728-9, but the last ones were not removed until the late eighteenth century when, after 1770, the park and the lake were extended. Part of the village site lies beneath the southern end of the lake. The inhabitants were systematically rehoused in new dwellings elsewhere on the estate at Longlands and, above all, at the Staithe which became the modern Holkham.

The Last Desertions?

Stanford, West Tofts and Tottington were three small villages in a sparsely inhabited part of Breckland. In 1942 the area was set aside as a 'live' military training ground. The inhabitants were evacuated at very short notice and the three sites have been deserted ever since, joining the long-deserted villages of Buckenham Tofts, Langford and Sturston. Their churches, with that of Langford, remain protected within their churchyards. Apart from a few earthworks marking the high-water extent of medieval settlement, the only other remains are grass-grown rubble mounds of more recent sites. At Tottington some empty buildings stand rebuilt for training in street fighting.

The evacuated villages had shown no signs of particular stress in medieval times. All experienced degrees of decline by the early fifteenth century, West Tofts faring rather better that the others, although Stanford had been granted a weekly market and an annual three-day fair in 1283. In 1404 the vicar of Tottington complained bitterly about the loss of his profits because of the depredations of rabbits from a neighbouring warren. By 1524 West Tofts appears to have been a community of comparatively wealthy people, while the other two remained on a par with villages nearby. The 1664 Hearth Tax shows only that West Tofts and Stanford were quite closely comparable. By the early twentieth century it was Tottington which had the largest population; all had declined since the mid-nineteenth century. Langford had been the least significant place by far in its hundred in 1334 but had at least 23 people paying Poll Tax in the 1370s. Clearly, something serious but as yet unknown happened as it had less than 10 households in 1428 and was allowed a large reduction of subsidy payment in 1449. It seems never to have recovered, and the few farms were evacuated in 1942.

Although some villages are continuing to flourish, others, less convenient for commuting and retirement, may decline. The mechanisation of farming has led to the amalgamation of farms and a reduction in the work force and it is possible to stumble across ploughed-out sites of tied cottages and small farmhouses as fields are walked. The sad relics of Eccles church and graveyard, scoured by the waves, remind us that the sea may claim more victims as sea levels rise. Another kind of erosion is seen in the closure and dilapidation of redundant churches, the selling of parsonage houses, the closure of village schools, shops, post offices and inns, and the withdrawal first of rail and then of bus services. Is the process of desertion really at an end?

THE PATTERN OF FUTURE RESEARCH

Filling in Blank Areas

Readers will have noticed that the detailed studies of desertion are drawn mainly from west and central Norfolk. This is because these are places where good earthworks have survived or where there are enough documents to tell the story.

Although deserted villages can certainly be found in eastern Norfolk they have left few surface traces. The more sprawling and scattered shapes of medieval villages in the south-eastern quarter have also served to conceal desertion. Quite often necessary documents are also missing. Bixley, south of Norwich, does have some good earthworks which have been surveyed but the documents which might explain them have not come to light. Just over its boundaries, in Arminghall, are striking but puzzling features under grass which are also a mystery. This is frustrating since these are the only impressive earthworks remaining in eastern Norfolk.

There is an obvious need to pick out and study a scattering of known or suspected sites in these less inviting 'empty quarters' and carry out field and documentary surveys.

Multi-Period Studies

While studies of single villages which have disappeared since medieval times have told us much that is useful, it is clear now that we would gain more by taking a wider view. Instead of studying the immediate surroundings of a suspected site, a bigger area such as the whole parish, or a larger block including neighbouring parishes, is chosen. A further step might be to take a more random area within a chosen district. This could be a large estate or simply a number of the kilometre squares shown on the OS map.

With the consent of landowners and farmers a surface survey is then made. All arable fields are systematically walked using a uniform method. This is usually done by walking back and forth at chosen intervals such as 10m, 20m or 30m until the whole field has been searched for surface finds of pottery, worked flints or metal objects. Areas of concentrated finds discovered in this way can then be searched more closely. After identification and recording, the patterns of finds of different periods can be plotted on maps, so showing the sequence of changes. Another more detailed method of survey is to divide each field into measured squares and search each in turn. In addition, all pastures and woods are searched for surviving earthworks which can then be mapped or plotted.

So far, a study of one group of three parishes - Loddon, Hales and Heckingham in south-east Norfolk - has been completed and published; others will follow. In the three parishes there was widespread evidence of prehistoric activity, though it seems to have been at its greatest in small valleys leading into the Chet with two notable sites on sandy knolls where worked flints and pottery of Late Neolithic and Early Bronze Age date have been found. Evidence from the Iron Age is disappointingly slight though it seems to have had some links with earlier sites and with some occupied in Romano-British times when there were many more sites on the lighter soils.

Early Saxon occupation of the three parishes appears sparse and was concentrated on three sandy knolls just above the small valleys, two of them having been exploited off and on since prehistoric days. But Middle Saxon times saw a distinct shift towards the valley of the Chet with marked activity near river crossings in Loddon and

Heckingham. Curiously, finds of neither period have been made in Hales.

Evidence of Late Saxon and Early Medieval settlement, recorded in its later stages in Domesday Book, had surprising features. Although a substantial number of people were recorded for Hales in 1086, they seem to have left very few signs of their presence - in direct contrast to Heckingham where activity had moved a little distance from the Middle Saxon sites. In the three parishes as a whole only small quantities of pottery of this period were found, either on sites or scattered over the fields, despite the Domesday evidence of intensive agriculture and a numerous population.

By the thirteenth century settlement had spread, extending to the edges of greens and riverside commons. Another feature was the appearance of what were probably isolated farmsteads away from the main centres. All of these were on lighter soils or on the very edges of heavier clays. The land at this time seems to have been heavily exploited, though signs of activity were much less on clays. Some low-lying sites were abandoned, probably because of rising water levels in Broadland. The late medieval settlement pattern was less strong with some sites abandoned and others shrinking considerably.

The value of this method is apparent in several ways. Patterns of settlement from different periods can be compared and considered. Although some places do seem to attract people over long periods of time, it is unlikely that they were occupied all the time. As settlers avoid unattractive places and choose those which are more desirable, the chances of sites of different periods coinciding, overlapping or being very near to one another are much greater.

The method also draws attention to shifts of activity and shows that places often moved slowly as time passed. It can also reveal long-forgotten farmsteads, hamlets and greenside settlements, distant from the main village, whose existence, even when good documents survive, is often unrecorded. Each parish may contain several deserted sites of differing periods; the deserted village is only a more prominent feature of a slow-changing overall pattern.

Similar studies of areas in west, central and north-eastern Norfolk are well advanced and it will soon be possible to compare them to see if there are regional differences in the way desertion occurred.

VISITING DESERTED VILLAGES

Of the very many deserted sites in Norfolk only a few still have impressive surface remains. Norfolk is an arable county and some went under the plough long ago. The pressures of two world wars and the development of modern farming practices have removed others in the present century.

Godwick is a surviving site at which there is a management agreement between the owner and English Heritage. The site, with its earthworks, is open to visitors between April and September from 9.30am until sunset. All that is required is that dogs must be kept on leads and that the Country Code be observed. Cars must be left in the farmyard in positions which will not impede farm traffic and the site has to be reached on foot along a marked route. On site there are information panels with displays of aerial and other photographs, maps and interpretation plans.

Godwick, until the fifteenth century, was a small village which was stable but comparatively poor alongside its neighbours. It declined sharply in that century, having under 10 households in 1428. A survey made in 1508 showed that, of 18 properties on the north side of the street, 11 were empty and three had no land attached. A mill, with its pond, and the church lay to the south. Further decay meant that, by 1595, Godwick had virtually gone. Its disappearance may have had more than one underlying cause. Its initial small size may have been due to its position on very heavy wet land which would have been difficult to cultivate under cooler, wetter conditions. The last stage of decline appears to have been accomplished by engrossment.

The earthworks of the medieval village compare well with a map of 1596 but changes were made by the building of a manor house in 1585 by Chief Justice Edward Coke and by the digging of clay pits. Part of the church tower survived a collapse in 1981. It had been largely rebuilt as a folly in the seventeenth century, but amongst the rubble of the fall was evidence of a Norman church.

Other Good Earthwork Sites

Earthworks can be seen elsewhere. Rights of way cross sites at Beachamwell All Saints and Harling Thorpe. Earthworks are partly visible from public roads at Pudding Norton, Great Palgrave, Roudham and Little Bittering, and from the churchyard at Bixley. Earthworks also survive at Egmere, Waterden and Rougham but cannot be seen from any public way. In all these cases further inspection can only be carried out with the permission of landowners and farmers.

DETECTING DESERTION

Although many deserted sites are already known, there must be more awaiting discovery. It is possible that 'humps and hollows' under surviving pastures may be the signs of former roads and buildings as shown in this diagram:

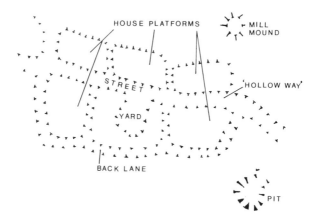

Aerial photographs may show such patterns in grassland or as crop or soil markings; the collection held by the Norfolk Museums Service may include evidence of this kind.

OS maps can give important pointers to deserted sites. Isolated or ruined churches, parishes without villages and the convergence of old footpaths and bridleways on apparently empty places are obvious clues. Strange projections in parish boundaries may show where the lands of defunct settlements have been added to those of the living.

Any investigation should begin with Blomefield's History of Norfolk. For articles and books written since, the Norfolk Bibliography should be consulted. In the present book many references have been made to Domesday Book, Lay Subsidies and Hearth Taxes and other sources. 'The Lost Villages of England' by Maurice Beresford (1954) will show how some of these can be used to tell the story of a desertion. 'The Lost Villages of Norfolk' by Keith Allison in Norfolk Archaeology (Vol XXXI, 116-162) shows how such methods were used to provide the first list of desertions for Norfolk. The Norfolk Record Office has many early maps and documents which may be consulted.

Reading On

For essential background information about the County of Norfolk 'The Norfolk Landscape' by David Dymond (1985), 'The Origins of Norfolk' by Tom Williamson (1993) and 'An Historical Atlas of Norfolk' edited by Peter Wade-Martins (2nd Edition 1994) should be consulted.

For further general reading 'Deserted Medieval Villages' by Maurice Beresford and John Hurst (1971) and 'Lost Villages of Britain' by Richard Muir (1982) are recommended. Detailed studies of some Norfolk desertions have been published in Norfolk Archaeology. The following East Anglian Archaeology Reports are important:

No 10 Village Sites in Launditch Hundred by Peter Wade-Martins.

No 14 includes studies of eight deserted villages in Norfolk by various authors.

No 44 Six Deserted Villages in Norfolk by Alan Davison and others.

No 46 The Deserted Medieval Villages of Thuxton, Norfolk by Lawrence Butler and Peter Wade-Martins.

No 49 The Evolution of Settlement in Three Parishes in South-east Norfolk by Alan Davison and Alayne Fenner.

No 51 The Ruined and Disused Churches of Norfolk by Neil Batcock.

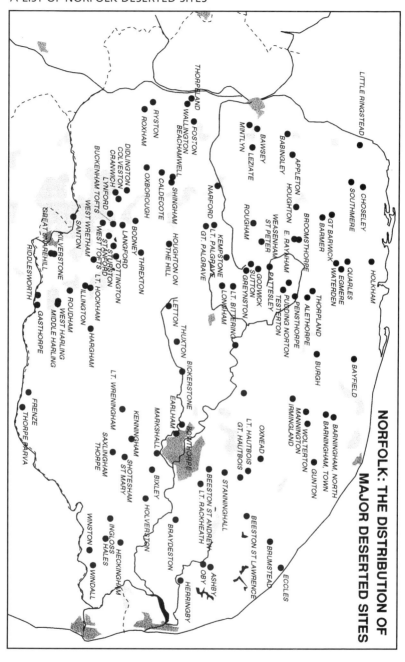

NORFOLK: THE DISTRIBUTION OF MAJOR DESERTED SITES

A LIST OF NORFOLK DESERTED SITES

This is not set out as a list of all deserted places but has been drawn up to include a wide geographical spread of varied sites. It owes much to the pioneering work of Keith Allison on Norfolk and to that of W Hudson, R Glasscock and J Sheail on Lay Subsidies, and to P Seaman and M Frankel on Hearth Taxes. Lay Subsidies were a series of medieval taxes which levied a proportion of the value of a man's movable goods (crops or stock). The amounts fixed in 1334 continued as a basis for taxation until the seventeenth century. Reductions were allowed to some places soon after the Black Death, and, because of economic decline, in 1449.

The following abbreviations are used in the notes:
DB   Domesday Book
NA   Norfolk Archaeology
EAA East Anglian Archaeology
NFA Norfolk from the Air
1332, 1334, 1449 and 1524 refer to Lay Subsidies and 1664 and 1666 to Hearth Taxes
1428 was the year in which exemption from a parish tax was granted to places having less than 10 households

Inclusion in this list does not imply public right of access.

GRID REFERENCES AND NOTES
Alethorpe (TF 948 313) See pp 46, 49-50,52, 73

Appleton (TF 705 274) DB church. 1334 combined with Flitcham. 1428 exempt. 1602 church decayed; Edward Paston, a noted Catholic recusant, was lord of all the lands. See EAA 51.

Ashby (TG 419 158) 1332, 1334 small. 1449 33% reduction. 1524 small, with Oby. Church site (cropmark) lies SE of Ashby Hall. See EAA 51. Oby is in the same parish.

Babingley (TF 670 263) 1332, 1334 substantial. 1449 21% reduction. 1602 church decayed. 1603 eight communicants only. 1611 land in hands of one lord. See EAA 51, NA XXXII.

A LIST OF NORFOLK DESERTED SITES

Barmer (TF 810 335) DB church. 1334 small. 1449 25% reduction. 1524 very small. 1664 one person only charged. If not strictly deserted, severely shrunken. Isolated church disused.

Barningham, North (Wood) (TG 151 372) DB substantial, not separate from Barningham, Town. 12thC separate. 1334 modest. 1449 24%+ reduction. 1524 small. 1745 two parishioners. See NA XXXIX, EAA 51.

Barningham, Town (Winter) (TG 147 357) See above. 1318 market. 1334 slightly better than B.N. 1449 15% reduction. 1524 small 1664 12 persons chargeable. 1797 map shows Hall, church but no park. Estate building?

Barwick, Great (TF 805 352) DB church. 1332/1334 modest size. Some reduction for Black Death. 1449 14% reduction. 1511 one parishioner. 1517 enclosure and decay reported.

Bawsey (TF 663 207) 1332/1334 small. 1428 exempt. 1449 14%+ reduction. 16thC enclosure by T Thursby. Fine church ruins. See EAA 51.

Bayfield (TG 050 405) 1332/1334 small. 1428 exempt. 1449 33% reduction. Church ruins near Hall in park.

Beachamwell (TF 752 054) See pp 10, 38, 42-44, 46 and EAA 44.

Beeston St Andrew (TG 251 146) DB church; five entries. 1334 modest.1449 13% reduction. 1524 very small. Church, site ploughed over, near Spixworth boundary. 1666 four persons chargeable (one for 15 hearths). 1797 map shows 'New Hall' and church demolished.

Beeston St Lawrence (TG 328 220) 1334 very small. 1428 exempt. 1449 57%+ reduction. Isolated church in use.

Bickerston (TG 086 087) DB insignificant. 1332/1334 very small. Some reduction after Black Death. 1449 45%+ reduction.

Bittering, Little (TF 935 175) See EAA 14. DB not separate from Great Bittering which lost its church early 16thC and has been subsumed by Gressenhall (TF 959 173)

Bixley (TG 257 040) See EAA 14.

Bodney (TL 831 989) 1334 moderate. 1449 17%+ reduction. 1524 small. Two moats, earthworks, fishponds. Isolated church still used. Late medieval/early post medieval desertion.

Bowthorpe (TG 177 091) 1334 small. Some reduction after Black Death. 1449 8%+ reduction. 1517 some enclosure and decay. 1522 destitute of parishioners. 1792 church abandoned, excavated 1985. See NFA.

Braydeston (TG 341 088) DB church. 1334/1449 combined with Strumpshaw. 1428 exempt. 1524 with Strumpshaw. Isolated church - site of village?

Broomsthorpe (TF 849 284) DB recorded. 1334 unmentioned. Poll Tax and 1524 with Tattersett. Tiny. Church abandoned early 16thC. Fine group of four fishponds.

Brumstead (TG 370 265) DB Church. 1334 moderate. 1449 9% reduction. 1524 one of smallest in hundred. 1664 15 persons chargeable. Church, Hall farm and large moat at centre of parish. If not deserted, typically shrunken.

Buckenham Tofts (TL 838 947) See pp 34, 65

Burgh (TG 044 335) DB unrecorded. 1334 small. Poll Tax 17 paid. 1428 exempt. 1449 10% reduction. 1524 very small. Mid 17thC, church abandoned.

Bylaugh (TG 036 184) 1334 quite prosperous. 1449 28%+ reduction. 1524 some decline shown? 1664 17 persons chargeable. 1845 only 85 people. No obvious cause of decline. See NFA.

Caldecote (TF 745 034) Site destroyed by ploughing. Church foundations on hill opposite farm. See EAA 10, NA XXXIX.

Choseley (TF 755 408) DB unrecorded. 1316 named with Little Ringstead. 1332/1334 quite tiny. Poll Tax: eight paid. 1428 exempt. 1449 44%+ reduction. 1517 enclosure, emparking, eviction and decay.

Colveston (TL 794 955) 1332/1334 tiny but apparently prosperous. 1428 exempt. 1449 8%+ reduction. Held by lords of Didlington 1402 onwards. 1524 combined with Ickburgh. 1676 church closed.

Cranwich (TL 783 949) 1334 rather small. 1449 10%+ reduction. 1524 relatively small. 1664 12 persons chargeable. Round-towered church in circular churchyard, signs of site nearby.

Didlington (TL 779 970) 1332/1334 quite substantial. 1449 11%+ reduction. 1524 decline shown. 17thC, purchasing-in. 18thC Hall, three or four houses, church only.

Earlham (TG 193 082) DB church. 1334 moderate. Some reduction after Black Death. 1449 31%+ reduction. 1524 very small. Hollow way in park.

Eccles (TG 414 288) Village of about 80 houses destroyed by sea by 1605. Fragments of church and other features sometimes revealed on shore. See NA XII and EAA 51.

Egmere (TF 897 374) See pp 35-38, 53, 70 EAA 14 and EAA 51.

Foston (Fodderstone) (TF 655 089) 1332/1334 very small. Some relief after Black Death. 1428 exempt. 1449 22%+ reduction. Church abandoned early 16thC.

Frenze (TM 135 804) 1332/1334 very small. 1428 exempt. 1524 very small. 1664 six persons charged. Church now disused.

Gasthorpe (TL 983 813) 1334 small. 1428 exempt. 1449 24% reduction. 1524 very small. Church abandoned by 18thC.

Godwick (TF 903 220) See p 69 EAA 14, 51 and NFA.

Greynston (Grenstein) (TF 907 198) Late settlement around green. DB unrecorded. Market grant 13thC. No church. Deserted 15thC. See EAA 10 and NFA.

Gunton (TG 230 340) 1334 small, survived to 1450 without apparent decline. 1524 still of fair standing. 1666 18 persons chargeable. 18thC emparking.

Hales (TM 380 960) DB substantial recorded population. 1334 small. Considerable relief after Black Death. 1449 20% reduction. 1524 small. Abandoned greenside settlement. Isolated Norman church. Modern village elsewhere. See pp 7, 18, 67-68 and EAA 49.

Hargham (TM 020 914) See pp 13, 31, 34, 56-58 and NA XXV.

Harling, Middle (TL 980 851) DB high valuation but declining by 1086. 1334 tiny. 1543 church demolished, foundations removed c1750. Important Middle Saxon site. See NA XXXVII and XXXVIII.

Harling, West (TL 975 852) See p 77   and NA XXXVII, XXXVIII, XLI.

Hautbois, Great (TG 262 204) DB not separated from Little. 1334 small. 1449 11%+ reduction. 1524 small. 1664 only eight persons chargeable. Fine ruined church and moated earthworks on site. See NA XXXIX and EAA 51.

Hautbois, Little (TG 251 218) DB see above. 1334 tiny. 1428 exempt. 1524 tiny. Church abandoned 16thC. Elizabethan Hall. Mayton Hall, opposite, may be the site of DB vill; it had a market charter in 1309.

Heckingham (TM 385 988) DB church, substantial recorded population. 1334 small. Some relief after Black Death. 1449 18%+ reduction. 1524 very small. Middle Saxon site near Norman church. Slow dispersal and late medieval shrinkage. See pp 5-6, 24, 67-68 and EAA 49.

Herringby (TG 446 103) 1332/1334 small but withstood 14th and early 15thC troubles. 1524 small. Church abandoned 16thC, demolished 1610.

Hockham, Little (TL 949 910) DB recorded, but not in subsequent national records. Archaeology: medieval expansion, survival to 16thC. See NA XL.

Holkham (TF 882 430) See pp 33, 35, 63-65 and EAA 44; 18thC emparking.

Holverston (TG 307 031) DB entries suggest subordinate status. Church mentioned in Anglo-Saxon will c.1057. 1334 small. 1428 exempt. 1449 26%+ reduction. 1524 tiny. Cropmark of round-towered church. See EAA 51.

Houghton (TF 794 285) See EAA 44; 18thC emparking. Some earthworks are in the park.

Houghton-on-the-Hill (TF 868 053) 1332/1334 moderately prosperous. 1449 26% reduction. 1524 tiny. 18thC no village. Church abandoned 1945.

Illington (TL 946 901) 1334 small, subsequently no obvious decline. 16th to early 17thC declining through engrossment. Disused church, Hall, few cottages. See p 12 and EAA 63.

Ingloss (TM 345 967) DB 'Golosa' with recorded population 19. Medieval decline to minor status in Loddon. Ingloss House. See EAA 49.

Irmingland (TG 123 294) 1332/1334 small. 1428 exempt. 1449 38%+ reduction. Church abandoned late 16thC.

Kempstone (TF 886 160) 1334 small. Some relief after Black Death; court roll shows mortality. 1381 insurgents looted property of Th. Clog. Poll Tax paid by 22. 1428 exempt. 1449 32%+ reduction. 1517 enclosure and small park. 1524 very small. Church still used late 19thC, now ruined. See EAA 10, 51.

Kenningham (TM 206 999) 1334 joined with Newton Flotman. Obscure history, united with Mulbarton 1452, when church demolished. Ill-defined site south of Kenningham Hall.

Kilverstone (TL 894 841) See pp 11, 31, 34, 56-57 and EAA 44.

Langford (TL 839 965) See p 65. Church survives, tower fell 1764.

Letton (TF 974 057) See pp 33, 62-63 and EAA 44.

Leziate (TF 695 199) DB insignificant. 1334 not listed. 1428 exempt. 1524 with Ashwicken. One of a group of desertions, probably another victim of Th. Thursby (16thC).

Longham (TF 935 155) Still exists but has two abandoned sites. See pp 17, 20 and EAA 10.

Lynford (TL 820 941) DB linked with Ickburgh. 1334 small. 1428 exempt. 1449 20% reduction. From 1467 church served by a monk from Thetford Cluniac Priory which then held the manor, the village being virtually empty. 19thC Hall and gardens.

Mannington (TG 144 320) DB substantial. 1332/1334 very small. 1449 almost 40% reduction. Hall built c1460. c1565 map shows no village, much land enclosed. Archaeology: Middle/Late Saxon activity near church, little medieval evidence. See NA XIV, NA XLII NFA.

Markshall (TG 228 047) DB substantial, church. 1332/1334 tiny, but no later reduction. Disappeared by 16thC? Batcock suggests depopulation due to proximity of Norwich. See NA XXX.

Mintlyn (TF 657 192) Lay Subsidies in 14thC: combined with Gaywood. 1524 small. 1664 10 persons chargeable. 1690 map shows 10 or 11 buildings and 'chapel'. A probable Thursby victim. See EAA 51.

Narford (TF 764 138) DB substantial. 1328 market. 1334 moderate prosperity. 1449 16%+ reduction. 1462 Survey shows some properties 'void'. 1578 further decay reported. 1664 12 chargeable. Early 18thC emparking.

Oby (TG 415 144) DB substantial. 1334 small but no subsequent reduction. 1524 with Ashby (see above). Church abandoned late 16thC.

Oxborough (TF 738 005) DB substantial. 1249 market. 1334 prosperous. 1449 37%+ reduction. 1524 prosperous. Grid ref is for Oxborough Hythe and remains of earlier church. Does this mark the original village? 1797 map shows some buildings just to the north. Compare with Methwold Hythe (TL 715 951) and Foulden St Edmund (TL 754 988).

Oxnead (TG 229 240) DB church. 1334 small. 1449 no reduction. 1478 Paston Letter: church small, no more than 20 receiving sacrament. 1524 very small. Service wing of Pastons' Hall survives.

Palgrave, Great (TF 834 120) DB three entries, largest as subordinate to Sporle; thereafter never separate. No church. Property of sheep farming lord looted 1381. See EAA 14.

Palgrave, Little (TF 832 135) DB not separated from above. 1254 church recorded. 1517 probably shared enclosure with above. Obscure history.

Pattesley (TF 899 241) DB recorded population of one! 1332/1334 very small. Poll Tax: 13 paid. 1428 exempt. 1449 no reduction. 1524 unlisted - disappeared by 16thC?

Pensthorpe (TF 947 290) Market by 1257. 1332/34 very small. Poll tax 19 paid. 1428 exempt. 1449 no reduction. 1524 unlisted. Disappeared by 16th C? 1603 10 communicants only.

Pudding Norton (TF 924 277) See pp 46, 51-53, 70 and EAA 14.

Quarles (TF 884 385) See pp 35, 37-38, 53 and EAA 51.

Rackheath, Little (About TG 277 132?) DB not separate from Rackheath. 1254 and 1368 church recorded. Rectors to 1407 then joined with Gt Rackheath.1428 exempt. Enclosure map: 'Chapel Close', a possible site?

Riddlesworth (TL 966 814) DB small. 1334 moderately prosperous. 1428 exempt. 1449 16%+ reduction. 1524 tiny. 1583 survey - manor house, church, rectory, 10 houses. 1672 Hearth Tax - manor and two houses charged. 1676 15 people. 17thC depopulation by Drurys?

Ringstead, Little (Barrett) (TF 684 399) DB not separate. 1332/1334 small. Black Death very large reduction made. 1428 exempt. 1449 21%+ reduction. 18thC: one farm. Possible extinction by pestilence. Church ruins remain.

Roudham (TL 956 872) 1334 substantial. Black Death some reduction allowed. 1449 27% reduction. 17thC - some wastage but extinguished by engrossment in 18thC. 1675: Ogilby's map shows small cluster well to east of church. See EAA 14, NFA.

Rougham (TF 825 207) See pp 9, 18, 23-24, 27, 38-42, 53, 70 and EAA 44.

Roxham (TL 638 997) DB insignificant. 1316 not recorded. 1334 unlisted. 1524 combined with West Dereham. 1566 map shows church but Batcock says it had been abandoned by 16thC. 17thC dispute over commons, sheep pastures and enclosures.

Ryston (TF 625 012) DB substantial. 1316 mentioned as distinct, afterwards combined with Bexwell for taxation. Small relief after Black Death. Probable emparking c1670. 18thC: reported depopulated. See NFA.

Santon (TL 828 873) 1334 small. 1428 exempt. 1449 19%+ reduction. 16thC handful of inhabitants. 17thC: tiny church built, enlarged 19thC. Large moat, medieval site to west under recreation area.

Saxlingham Thorpe (TM 230 966) DB not distinguished in extensive entries. Lay Subsidies: not separated. Named settlement still exists away from considerable ruins of church. Site, up to medieval times, N of church: a good example of shifting. See EAA 51.

Shingham (TF 762 052) DB insignificant. 1334/1449 not listed. 1428 exempt. 1524 with Beachamwell. 1664 nine persons chargeable. If not deserted severely shrunken. See EAA 51.

Shotesham St Mary (TM 238 988) DB Shotesham and 'other' Shotesham, 14 entries, two churches. St Mary (standing) has two other churches - St Martin (ruins) and St Botolph (foundations). St Botolph and St Martin recorded before 1066. 1311 St Botolph and St Mary united. 1334 'Shotesham' (all) very prosperous. 1428 St Mary,

St Martin both exempt. 1449 22%+ reduction. 1517 some enclosure, deprivation of grazing rights. 1524 (All Shoteshams combined) large. 1664 (St Mary) 22 persons chargeable.

Snarehill, Great (TL 893 835)   DB one of two 'Snarehills'. 1316 'Snarehill' alone. 1334 very small. Poll Tax: 32 paid in 'Snarehill'. 1428 exempt. 1449 33% reduction. Church repairs recorded early 16thC. Remains of church in stables at Hall. DB 'Alia' Snarehill probably at TL 887 810, remains of possible church reported, 1908, nearby. See EAA 51.

Stanford (TL 855 946) See pp 56, 65-66

Stanninghall (TG 255 175) DB belonged in Horstead. 1334/1449 unlisted probably with Horstead. 16thC surveys show 'Stanninghall Field'. Church ruined by 1602, having had a Catholic lord and patron. Ruins at Stanninghall Farm.

Sturston (TL 875 950) See pp 46, 53-56, 65.

Summerfield (Southmere) (TF 748 385) DB substantial. 1332/1334 small. 1428 exempt. 1449 28% reduction. 16thC church and village probably gone. Now a tiny hamlet in Docking.

Sutton (TF 895 206) DB 'Suttuna'. Grew beside Tittleshall; both Middle Saxon in origin. Early medieval decline. See EAA 10.

Tattersett (TF 850 293) DB two churches. 1334 prosperous. 1428 parish of Tattersett St Andrew exempt. 14499 15% reduction. St Andrew abandoned early 16thC. 1666 13 charged. Earthworks near isolated All Saints' and also around the foundations of St Andrew's.

Testerton (TF 937 267) 1329/1334 modest. Black Death no relief. 1428 exempt. 1449 31%+ reduction. 1517 some enclosure reported. 1602 church decayed, sole lord was Catholic. Batcock says church abandoned c1680, ruins near Testerton House.

Thorpe Parva (TM 161 794) 1332/1334 tiny. Black Death no relief. 1428 exempt. 1449 16%+ reduction. 1517 decay of church and some houses. 1602 Church completely ruined c1540 by a Mr Doyly. Round tower remains.

Thorpland (TF 616 083) DB substantial, church. 1334 very small, with Wallington. 1449 20% reduction (again combined) 1524, with Wallington again, small. Church abandoned end of 15thC. 1845 two farms, five cottages.

Thorpland (TF 937 322) See pp 46-50, 52.

Threxton (TF 885 001) 1332/1334 moderately prosperous. Black Death: no relief. 1449 11%+ reduction. 1524 small. Probable victim of engrossment. Church still intact.

Thuxton (TG 035 075) DB records TURSTUNA, TURSTANTUNA, two places, still distinct in 1212. 1334, one place, moderately prosperous. Black Death: some relief. Poll Tax: 38 paid. 1449 25% reduction. 1524 small, and slow decline continued. See EAA 46.

Tofts, West (TL 837 928) See p 65 and EAA 51.

Tottington (TL 893 955) See pp 55-56, 65.

Wallington (TF 626 076) DB substantial, church. 1334/1449/1524 see Thorpland. Judge Gawdy depopulated it to make a park, destroying the church, save for the tower. Dying in 1606, he had to be hastily buried elsewhere. See EAA 51.

Waterden (TF 887 364) See pp 9, 35-37, 53, 70 and EAA 14.

Weasenham St Peter (TF 856 224) DB not separated from Weasenham All Saints. 1334 not separate, prosperous. 1449 not separate, 8% reduction. 1664 (W St P) c24 persons chargeable. Archaeology: shows clear migration from original site. See EAA 10.

Windall (Windle) (about TM 427 939) DB unrecorded. 1334 tiny. 1428 exempt. 1449 26%+ reduction. Church abandoned c1440. 1524 tiny. Location? Windle Hill?

Winston (TM 401 931) DB unrecorded. 1334 tiny. 1428 exempt.1449 nearly 54% reduction. 15thC: church abandoned. 1524 tiny.

Witchingham, Little (TG 117 204) 1334 well below average. Black Death: moderate relief given. 1449 10%+ reduction, smaller than the average. 1524 had become small and poor. 1664 eight persons only chargeable.

Wolterton (TG 164 324) DB church. 1332/1334 small, well below average. Poll Tax: 37 paid. 1449 23%+ reduction 1524 small. 1732: map shows small settlement around rectangular green. Archaeology confirms medieval origin of this. Emparked soon after. Parish Register suggests church occasionally used to 1780, tower only remains. See NA XLII

Wreningham, Little (About TM 155 980) DB records 'Vrnincham' and 'Neilanda'. c1050 Naylond and Wreningham churches recorded. 1406 Little Wreningham church (St Mary) united with Naylond. 1414 Naylond added to Wreningham. Where are these places? A fine mystery to solve.

Wretham, West (TL 900 914) DB three Wrethams recorded. 1334 moderate, a little below average. Poll Tax: 31 paid. No reductions after Black Death or in 1449. 1524 rather poor and small. 17thC engrossment. 1793: church closed, all but two houses demolished, people moved to East Wretham. Emparking. Little Wretham (Thorpe) is a minor deserted site here.

Index

INDEX

INDEX

INDEX

INDEX